Ben Franklin

What People are Saying about *Ben Franklin: America's Original Entrepreneur*

"Franklin's autobiography is America's first great self-help book. It teaches in a delightful way how to win friends, influence people, and succeed in business. Professor McCormick makes this great work more accessible and adds his own insights."

—WALTER ISAACSON, AUTHOR, *BENJAMIN FRANKLIN: AN AMERICAN LIFE*

"Anyone who's got the bug and drive to become a great leader and innovator can only be inspired by the life of Benjamin Franklin, who quite literally wrote the book for getting the most out of himself and bringing out the best in others. His genius—scientific, entrepreneurial, diplomatic, and literary—was *sui generis*. His *Autobiography* is a classic of American letters, and he emerges from the pages of Professor McCormick's version not only as our contemporary, but also as a 21st century visionary, not to mention a wise companion."

—DR. JUDITH RODIN, PRESIDENT EMERITA, THE UNIVERSITY OF PENNSYLVANIA
AND PRESIDENT, THE ROCKEFELLER FOUNDATION

"Statesman and inventor are the first images that come to mind when we think of Benjamin Franklin, but as his autobiography will remind us, he was also a very successful entrepreneur and a most fascinating individual. Dr. McCormick brings the story of Franklin's entrepreneurial spirit alive for today's audience in his adaptation of Franklin's autobiography."

—UNITED STATES CONGRESSMAN MICHAEL N. CASTLE (DELAWARE),
FIFTH GENERATION FRANKLIN DESCENDANT

"After reading this book, you'll understand why Ben Franklin means business. McCormick conveys the essence of American entrepreneurial spirit embodied by one of America's most skillful citizens."

—ROY GOODMAN, ACTING PRESIDENT, FRIENDS OF FRANKLIN AND
MEMBER OF THE AMERICAN PHILOSOPHICAL SOCIETY, FOUNDED BY FRANKLIN

"One of the most fascinating and least examined aspects of Franklin's life is that of his entrepreneurship and great success as a businessman. Amazingly, the skills he developed are still relevant to the business world today. Blaine has captured the essence of Franklin's model for success and shares it in a way that allows all of us to examine, learn from, and prosper by Franklin's wisdom. Read this only if you want to energize your life."

—RALPH ARCHBOLD, OFFICIAL BEN FRANKLIN FOR THE CITY OF PHILADELPHIA

Ben Franklin

America's Original Entrepreneur

Franklin's Autobiography for Business Today
Adapted by Blaine McCormick

EP
Entrepreneur
Press

Jere L. Calmes, Publisher
Cover design: Perlman & Peterson Design
Composition and production: Eliot House Productions

This publication is designed to provide accurate and authoritative information in regard to the
subject matter covered. It is sold with the understanding that the publisher is not engaged in
rendering legal, accounting, or other professional services. If legal advice or other expert
assistance is required, the services of a competent professional person should be sought.

Library of Congress Cataloging-in-Publication Data
McCormick, Blaine.
 Ben Franklin: America's original entrepreneur/by Blaine McCormick.
   p. cm.
 ISBN-13: 978-1-59918-195-0 (alk. paper)
 ISBN-10: 1-59918-195-9 (alk. paper)
  1. Franklin, Benjamin, 1706–1790. 2. Statesmen—United States—Biography.
 3. Scientists—United States—Biography. 4. Printers—United States—Biography.
 5. Inventors—United States—Biography. 6. Businesspeople—United States—Biography.
 7. Entrepreneurship—United States—Case studies. I. Title.
 E302.6.F8M124 2008
 973.3092—dc22
  [B]   2008004708

Printed in Canada

12 11 10 09 08   10 9 8 7 6 5 4 3 2 1

Table of Contents

PART I

The Making of an Entrepreneur

PART II

The Rise of an Entrepreneur

PART III

The Legacy of an Entrepreneur

Foreword

SO MUCH IS KNOWN ABOUT BENJAMIN FRANKLIN as founding father, framer, statesman, scientist, philosopher, author, master of the epigram, and fount of earthy wisdom that it is small wonder we have little room left for recognition of his talents as entrepreneur and businessman. This recognition is much needed and long overdue. With all of his other talents, this great patriot also qualifies as the first American entrepreneur.

Perhaps the delay in the recognition of Franklin's entrepreneurial talent has arisen from a misunderstanding of what entrepreneurship is all about. While in today's grand era of capitalism the word "entrepreneur" has come to be commonly associated with those who are motivated to create new enterprises largely by the desire for personal wealth or even greed, the fact is that the most basic definition of entrepreneur is "one who undertakes an enterprise," a person who founds and directs an organization.

There is a difference, then, between an entrepreneur and a capitalist. Had Franklin possessed the soul of a true capitalist, the time he saved from his successful printing business would likely have been invested in making money somewhere else. But for him, the getting of money was always a means to an end, not the end in itself. When he reminded us that "energy and persistence conquer all things," Franklin was likely describing his own motivations to create and to succeed.

The enterprises he created and the things he invented were designed for the public weal, not for personal profit. Consider Franklin's greatest creations: The Colonies' first fire company; the nation's oldest property insurance company, still thriving today; the Franklin stove, whose stunning efficiencies slashed families' heating costs; and the lightning rod; along with a library, a hospital, and a college (now the University of Pennsylvania). Now there is one truly eclectic entrepreneur!

These creations reflect Dr. Franklin's inspiring 18th-century version of entrepreneurship. They reflect the applications of his relentless energy and persistence to the service of the community's greater good; his invention—largely through trial and error and common sense—of devices that would improve the community's quality of life; and his view that virtue is not only achievable by us mortals, but is the principal requirement of a life well-lived. For Franklin, "knowledge was not the personal property of its discoverer, but the common property of all. As we enjoy great advantages from the inventions of others," he wrote, "we should be glad of an opportunity to serve others by any invention of ours, and this we should do freely and generously."

Even viewed through the lens of 21st-century cynicism rather than 18th-century idealism, I confess a sense of wonder at the young Franklin's moral strength and disciplined self-improvement. While virtue is a word that tends to embarrass us today, it surely didn't embarrass Dr. Franklin. In 1728, when he was but 22 years of age, he tells us that he, "conceived the bold and arduous project of arriving at moral perfection . . . I knew, or thought I knew, what was right and wrong, and I did not see why I might not always do the one or avoid the other." The task, he tells us, was more difficult than he imagined, but he ultimately listed 13 virtues—including *Temperance, Silence, Frugality, Industry, Sincerity, and Justice*—and attempted to honor them in his own life.

While few of us in today's society would have the will to pursue a written agenda of virtue, Franklin had established, in his own words, the "character of Integrity" that would give him so much influence with his fellow citizens in the struggle for American independence. Wrapped in integrity and virtue, his character was also central to his dedication to the public interest. It is in that sense that his true entrepreneurship emerges. Franklin took joy from his creations and from exercising his ingenuity, his energy, and his persistence. Franklin sought not the fruits of success, but success for its own sake, exercising his talents with a view not toward personal gain and private profit, but toward serving the community. "America's first entrepreneur" may well be our finest one.

History honors Benjamin Franklin as an American icon, one of the most important of the Founding Fathers, a central participant in the drafting of both the Declaration of Independence and the Constitution, and a signer of both. But today, through his candid and idealistic autobiography and through his enlightened entrepreneurship, Franklin seems less iconic and more approachable, a humble human being who embodies, as well as any of the Signers, what have come to be known as the bulwarks of the American character.

—John C. Bogle, founder and former chief executive
of The Vanguard Group

INTRODUCTION

The Founding Father of American Business

SOMETIME DURING THE LAST 50 YEARS MOST OF us stopped reading *The Autobiography of Benjamin Franklin* even though it's one of the greatest success stories in American history. Twenty-first century readers picking up Franklin's autobiography find it a challenging read for a number of reasons. Though written in English, the language is noticeably dated at this point and Franklin doesn't always conform to our modern rules of grammar. Because Franklin wrote his autobiography in multiple settings, the text is also characterized more by fragmentation than consistency. Beyond this, the colonial context in which Franklin lived and worked is less and less familiar to the average reader. There are just too many changes across two centuries of capitalism.

Contrary to perceptions people might have of him, Franklin fully expected his autobiography to be more useful to young businesspeople than to, say, budding diplomats or scientists. In a letter he wrote about 18 months prior to his death, Franklin noted that his autobiography ". . . will be of more Use to young Readers; as exemplifying the Effect of prudent and imprudent Conduct in the Commencement of a Life of Business." Franklin clearly wanted the book to be useful to those interested in a career in business, and it is in this spirit that I have modernized his original text. Franklin's autobiography remains one of the greatest works in American literature, and it has influenced generations of businesspeople both in the United States and abroad.

American business operates in a competitive, market-driven economy. As a result, businesspeople have looked to competitively-minded texts like Machiavelli's *The Prince* or Sun Tzu's *The Art of War* for insight. In fact, if one were to review the titles on the business shelf at virtually any bookstore, one would discover that these two texts have spawned a cottage industry of books, including offerings like *The Mafia Manager: A Guide to the Corporate Machiavelli* and *Applying Sun Tzu's Art of War in Customer Service*. It's time we stopped looking to the East or to the West for management wisdom. Americans have their own homegrown business guru: Benjamin Franklin. He did nothing less than capture the cultural DNA of American capitalism at its beginning and pass it on to readers for all time. This is not only business history but also our entrepreneurial heritage.

Most people are familiar with Franklin's business counsel through the wise and witty sayings in his best-selling *Poor Richard's Almanac*. Maxims like "God helps those who help themselves" and "Early to bed and early to rise make a man healthy, wealthy, and wise" have become deeply ingrained parts of American culture enjoyed by people in both colonial and modern times (and I've included one of these quotes in every chapter). This book is written to give modern readers a fuller understanding of the man whose wisdom they have long enjoyed and heeded.

In contrast to his almanacs, Franklin wrote his autobiography as a book of stories. Sayings like "Haste makes waste" are memorable, but stories give a much richer context to a person's life and allow for more complexity. Many of the stories can be viewed as morality tales, and sometimes it's Franklin who learns the valuable lesson. Maybe the greatest contribution Franklin made with his autobiography was giving us the true story of business success. Is the formula for business success "lie, cheat, steal, and bully," or is it something closer to "early to bed and early to rise"?

Franklin uses his autobiography to promote such virtues as honesty, hard work, thrift, doing good to others, and having a good reputation. He more often than not utilizes the power of reward in getting others to cooperate rather than relying on the power of punishment. As such, Franklin is an ideal role model for learning the art of what is commonly known as "mixed-motive exchange."

That is, businesspeople often feel a tension between their desire to compete and their desire to cooperate in any given business situation. Franklin admirably manages this tension and throughout the autobiography shows us how to compete and cooperate at the same time. He protects his interests and guards against foolish risks while at the same time helping others around him to succeed. Rather than dominate the game as per Machiavelli or Sun Tzu, he shows us how to lift the boats of those around him—as well as his own.

Why I Wrote this Book

My goal in this adaptation is to make Franklin's amazing story accessible to the modern business reader. First and foremost, I've broken the autobiography into 82 chapters and updated both the language and syntax. In addition, I've rearranged some of Franklin's stories so that they appear in their proper chronological order and corrected a few of Franklin's minor recall errors. Finally, I've also removed a few parts that were either repetitious or did not add significant value for the modern reader interested in Franklin's business story.

This book divides Franklin's autobiography into three major parts. The first part details his upbringing and explains the lessons he learned on his way to becoming a businessowner. It covers the first 20 years of Franklin's life, from 1706 through the summer of 1726. The second part deals primarily with Franklin's years as a printer in Philadelphia and concludes when he retires from his business in 1748. The third part showcases a highly effective Franklin moving into the public arena and applying his business knowledge to civic projects, military efforts, and diplomacy. Part III carries Franklin's story through the summer of 1757, when politics and diplomacy begin to dominate his life.

One will have to look elsewhere for Franklin's complete autobiography in its original arrangement and vernacular. On that note, nothing would please me more than to discover that reading this book helped you return to Franklin's original text to study it with greater appreciation.

For Miriam and Beatrice

PART I

The Making of an Entrepreneur

CHAPTER 1

Why Bother Writing Your Own Story?

In the summer of 1771, the 65-year-old Franklin enjoyed an unusually long vacation during which he spent two weeks in England at the home of Dr. Jonathan Shipley, Bishop of St. Asaph's. He began writing his autobiography there. Franklin had already lived a remarkable life by anyone's standards—even before the additional fame that would come to him during the Revolutionary War. He begins his memoirs by sharing his purpose for writing. Namely, since he can't live his life over again, maybe those who read his story will have the chance to imitate his successes and avoid his failures. On a larger note, the autobiography itself is one of Franklin's greatest successes and our first challenge from him. What stories and advice will you leave behind for those who follow after you?

I'VE ALWAYS TAKEN GREAT PLEASURE IN HEARING or reading stories about my ancestors. During a visit to England in 1757, I gathered a number of such stories from my living relatives. Since people are largely unfamiliar with the story of my life, and they might also find such stories interesting, I sit down to write them during these two weeks of uninterrupted leisure in the English countryside.

I have other reasons for writing these memoirs in addition to informing people of my ancestry. I was born and raised in America in poverty and obscurity and have achieved considerable wealth, fame, and happiness thus far in life. People may one day wish to know exactly how—with the blessings of God—I arrived at this state of wealth, fame, and happiness and may even wish to adopt and imitate some of my methods and habits.

As I reflect on my current happiness, I can honestly say that if I were given the opportunity to live my life over again from the beginning I would do so. Having been a printer, I would only ask to have the editorial advantage of being able to correct the faults of the first edition of my life during the second edition. I would also welcome the opportunity to avoid accidentally harming some of the people I did along the way, now having the benefit of hindsight. Nonetheless, even if both requests were denied, I would still accept the offer.

Since one can never really repeat one's life, the next best thing one can do is to remember one's life and make that remembrance as permanent as possible by putting it down in writing. As old men are fond of talking of both themselves and their own past actions, I hope to accomplish this without boring others.

POOR RICHARD ONCE SAID, "IF YOU WOU'D NOT BE FORGOTTEN AS SOON AS YOU ARE DEAD AND ROTTEN, EITHER WRITE THINGS WORTH READING, OR DO THINGS WORTH THE WRITING."

Younger people who—because of my age—might otherwise feel obliged to listen to my stories when I tell them can stop reading whenever they wish, without fear of offending me.

Finally, I may as well admit this upfront, as it's difficult to deny in any credible way: Writing this autobiography might gratify a good deal of my own vanity. Most people dislike displays of self-importance in others, despite doing a good bit of it themselves. I've scarcely ever heard or seen the phrase, "Without the least bit of vanity let me say..." but some self-promoting story immediately followed. Thus, I try to give vanity due credit whenever I encounter it, as it can sometimes benefit not only the possessor, but also others who fall within his circle of influence. As such, it would not be altogether absurd if someone were to thank God for their vanity since even it can make the world a better place from time to time.

Speaking of thanksgiving, with all humility I wish to acknowledge that I would have experienced none of the abovementioned happiness had God not led me to the right path and given me success once upon it. My belief in such guidance leads me to hope (but never assume) that this same goodness will continue to bless me and either continue my happiness or strengthen me to bear the difficult times that can come upon any person. God alone knows my future, and He can bless us even in our troubles.

Businesspeople throughout American history have followed Franklin's example by writing down the story of their lives and businesses for others to read. Some 20th century examples include Alfred Sloan (*My Years with General Motors*), Lee Iacocca (*Iacocca: An Autobiography*), Berry Gordy (*Movin' Up: Pop Gordy Tells His Story*), Mary Kay Ash (*Mary Kay*), and Michael Dell (*Direct from Dell*).

CHAPTER 2

Franklin Means Freedom

Reaney's Dictionary of English Surnames notes that "Franklin" is derived from the Middle English word "frankeleyn," meaning "a free-man, a land-owner of free but not noble birth." Franklin had freedom in his blood, so to speak. In this chapter, Franklin discusses his ancestors and tells of how they celebrated their freedom by rebelling against authority in their choice of religion. He also notes that he was the youngest son of the youngest son for five generations back in his family. In a landowning aristocracy, he would be doomed to inherit nothing. In the American colonies, by contrast, he could by dint of his own effort become a wealthy citizen.

One of my uncles who also enjoyed collecting stories about the family gave me some detailed notes about my ancestry. From these writings I learned that my family had lived in the same village, Ecton, in Northhamptonshire, for at least 300 years—maybe longer, but we don't know for sure. About three centuries ago, people all over the kingdom assumed surnames, and our clan assumed the name "Franklin." The family lived on about 30 acres, which they owned free and clear. In addition to the land, the family had maintained a blacksmith's business for many generations with the eldest son always being trained to continue the business—a custom that my own father, a candle maker, followed with his eldest son. When I searched the records at Ecton, I found details of the family's births, marriages, and burials all the way back to the year 1555. Prior to this date, no records were kept. Reading these records, I learned that I was the youngest son of the youngest son for five generations back.

My grandfather, Thomas, was born in 1598 and lived in Ecton until he grew too old to keep up with his business. He then moved to Banbury, in Oxfordshire, to live with his son John, a wool dyer, under whom my father would apprentice. My grandfather died in Banbury, and I visited his grave during my time there in 1758. His eldest son, also named Thomas, remained in the house at Ecton which he left along with the land to his only child, a daughter. She and her husband sold the place, but the new owner has kept it in excellent condition.

My grandfather had four sons that survived childhood. Their names were Thomas, John, Benjamin, and Josiah. According to family tradition, Thomas was trained to be a blacksmith like his father. However, being rather intelligent and encouraged to further study by one of the leading citizens, he became a document clerk. This resulted in his becoming a leading citizen in both the county of Northampton and his own village. He achieved a small degree of fame for his many public projects, some supported by Lord Halifax. He died on January 17, 1702—four years to the day before I was born. As our lives have had certain parallels, some family members half-believe that there was a transmigration of soul from his body to mine.

> POOR RICHARD ONCE SAID, "A FINE GENIUS IN HIS OWN COUNTRY, IS LIKE GOLD IN THE MINE."

As I mentioned earlier, John became a dyer of wools. Benjamin, in contrast, became a silk dyer, serving an apprenticeship in London. He was an intelligent man, like his oldest brother, Thomas. I knew Benjamin personally as he traveled to our home in Boston when I was a young boy and lived there several years. He lived to a very old age, and his grandson, Samuel Franklin, now lives in Boston. When he died, Benjamin left behind two books of poetry, which he had written for friends and family. He invented his own method of shorthand writing which he taught me. I never practiced it, however, and have now forgotten it. Because he and my father were so close, my father chose to name me after this uncle.

My uncle Benjamin was very religious and listened often to the best preachers, writing down each of their sermons in his special shorthand. He was also fascinated by politics, although he never had the resources to pursue a public life. His interest was to such a degree that he had almost a complete collection of political pamphlets dating from 1641 to 1717 (when he left for America). Much to my surprise, his collection was shown to me by a dealer of old books when I was in London many years later. Apparently, he left them there when he departed, and I learned a good deal about him by reading the notes he left in the margins.

This little-known family of ours became Protestants early in the Reformation and remained so through the reign of Queen Mary. They were often in danger as they countered her zeal for the Catholic Church with their own zeal against it. Being Protestants, they were rebellious and had obtained their own Bible, which they fastened open with straps to the underside of a stool. My uncle Benjamin told me that my great-great grandfather would turn the stool up on his knees when reading the Bible to his family, keeping the pages neatly fastened under a set of straps. While he read, one of the children stood watch at the door to warn if an officer of the spiritual court should appear on patrol. Should this happen, the stool could quickly be turned down upon its feet, concealing the Bible without losing the place of the reading.

All the brothers remained with the Church of England until near the end of the reign of Charles II, when some of the Church's ministers were removed for disregarding the Church hierarchy and worshipping in a way of their own choosing. My father and his brother Benjamin chose to follow these nonconformist ministers. The rest of the family remained affiliated with the Church of England and embraced the dictates of its authorities.

Franklin was not the only Founding Father who succeeded in business. Fellow Philadelphians George Clymer and Robert Morris were both well-known merchants. Morris would found the Bank of North America. John Langdon was a New Hampshire merchant who commanded his own trade ship for a time. Nathaniel Gorham was a self-made businessman from Massachusetts. Roger Sherman, also of Massachusetts, began as a shoemaker, became a merchant, and ultimately set up his own law practice.

CHAPTER 3

Credit to Whom Credit Is Due

Contrary to perceptions of Franklin being a "self-made man," he gives due credit in these opening chapters to God and others for aiding the successes of his life. Franklin acknowledged his forebears of three centuries in the previous chapter. Here he recognizes his father and mother for influencing him. He clearly viewed himself as part of a social network to which he had some obligation to reciprocate later in life. This reciprocation would take a variety of forms, including his many public projects.

MY FATHER, JOSIAH, MARRIED YOUNG AND, along with his wife and three children, crossed the Atlantic to New England in 1683. With their religious gatherings forbidden by law and frequently interrupted, Josiah and many of his acquaintances decided to go elsewhere in search of religious freedom.

Father and his first wife had four more children after their arrival in New England. When she died, he took a second wife and they had ten more. In all, father sired 17 children. Almost all of them survived to adulthood and married. I recall

13 of them gathered around his table at one time. I was the youngest son—born in Boston—and only two more children were born after me.

My mother, father's second wife, was Abiah Folger, daughter of one of the first settlers of New England, Peter Folger. If I recall correctly, no less than Cotton Mather makes honorable mention of Folger as a "godly, learned Englishman" in his history of churches in New England. From time to time Folger wrote short poems, and I saw one of them printed many years ago. In 1675 he addressed one of his poems to his Puritan neighbors concerned about their government. The piece favored liberty of conscience and attributed the Indian wars and other civil distresses to Divine judgment on the country. Such judgments, Folger contended, could be lessened by repealing the laws that persecuted the Baptists, the Quakers, and other religious sects. The piece was plainly and courageously written and concluded with a statement of goodwill from the author, who refused to remain anonymous.

Father was always healthy, of average height, but well proportioned and very strong. He was both intelligent and had a talent for drawing. He displayed a strong mechanical talent and could master many tradesmen's tools when he had need. In addition, he had a wonderful singing voice and played a variety of musical instruments. Sometimes at the end of a business day, he played hymns on his violin and sang along with them. These times remain a pleasant memory.

Franklin begins his autobiography by giving thanks to God and family; then he talks about his business. Mary Kay Ash had the same priorities when she founded Mary Kay Cosmestics. She made it clear to everyone in her company that their priorities should be: "God first, family second, career third."

Father's supreme talent lay in his sensible wisdom and solid judgment in both private and public conflicts. He could never become a judge, given his large family and the necessities of running the family business. Nonetheless, I remember many occasions when leading citizens visited our home to seek his opinion regarding the affairs of the town or church. His counsel was always heeded, and many of these people returned to seek counsel about matters more private. When conflict flared, father was frequently chosen to arbitrate the affair in lieu of the two parties going to court.

We often had some levelheaded friend or neighbor join us at our table where he and father would invariably engage in clever or useful conversation intended to be overheard by the children. In this way, father educated us to the good, the just, and the sensible things of life. I've since learned that other families talked incessantly at the table about what food was being served, whether it tasted good or looked attractive, or whether or not it was preferable to something else that might have been served. As a result of my upbringing, I maintain few opinions as to matters of food and remain so unobservant of my meals that I can barely remember what I ate within a few hours of mealtime. I've concluded that this ignorance has served me well in traveling, as I often dine with companions of more educated tastes and appetites and regularly find them in a state of dissatisfaction.

My mother was as healthy as father, as demonstrated by her nursing all ten of her children. Neither of them had a day of serious illness in all their lives until the illnesses that took their lives. Father died at age 89 and mother died at age 85. They now lie buried together in Boston, where some years ago I placed a gravestone with this inscription:

> POOR RICHARD ONCE SAID, "THINK OF THREE THINGS, WHENCE YOU CAME, WHERE YOU ARE GOING, AND TO WHOM YOU MUST ACCOUNT."

JOSIAH FRANKLIN,

and

ABIAH his Wife,

lie here interred.

They lived lovingly together in wedlock

fifty-five years.

Without an estate, or any gainful employment,

By constant labor and industry,

with God's blessing,

They maintained a large family comfortably,

and brought up thirteen children

and seven grandchildren

reputably.

From this instance, reader,

Be encouraged to diligence in thy calling,

And distrust not Providence.

He was a pious and prudent man;

She, a discreet and virtuous woman.

Their youngest son,

In filial regard to their memory,

Places this stone.

J.F. born 1655, died 1744, age 89.

A.F. born 1667, died 1752, age 85.

CHAPTER 4

The Enduring Legacy of Moral Instruction

Key parts of Franklin's personality begin to emerge in this chapter: a love of reading, an affinity for leadership, and a bias for action. Franklin also tells about his early work and his minimal education. In addition, his father bemoans the high cost of a college education, reminding us that some things have never changed in America. The chapter ends with what may very well be the first great lesson in the young Franklin's life: the necessity for honesty in all endeavors. An honest reputation was the foundation on which he built his business enterprises, and the reader will notice the theme recurring again and again throughout the autobiography.

MY OLDER BROTHERS WERE ALL APPRENTICED to different trades. In contrast, I was sent to Boston's Free Latin School when I was eight years old. Being the last of ten sons, my father decided to devote me, as a tithe, to the service of the Church. His decision was influenced, in part, by my learning to read very early in life. In fact, I can't recall a time when I could not read. Furthermore, it was the opinion of all his friends that I would do well in studies. My uncle Benjamin approved of the decision and promised to give me the many volumes in which he had copied down sermons in his special shorthand. Were I to commit to learn his special shorthand characters, a windfall of sermons would be mine as I began my calling in the Church.

I stayed at the Latin school not quite one year. During that time, I not only rose to the head of my class, but I advanced into the class ahead of me. My father, however, changed his mind about my education. Given the size of his family, the cost of a college education, and the distinct possibility of my getting a low-paying job after graduation, he removed me from Latin school. I continued my studies at a school for penmanship and arithmetic led by a reputable educator, Mr. George Brownell, who educated by means of mild and encouraging methods. Under his oversight, I quickly mastered writing but failed miserably in arithmetic.

At ten years old I was taken home to assist my father in his business. He found little demand for his dying trade when he arrived in New England, and so he retrained himself as a soap and candle maker. He employed me in a variety of tasks, including cutting the wicks for candles, filling the molds, attending the shop, and running errands.

Finding the work dull and repetitive, I preferred the life of a sailor to that of a candle maker, but my father refused to let me go to sea. Since we lived near the water, though, I learned to swim very early in my life and also to manage boats. When using a boat or a canoe with other boys, I often found myself in a leadership role, especially in the event of a crisis. I tried to be a good leader among my friends, but I sometimes led them into trouble. Let me share one story with you of an episode that was not conducted in an entirely ethical manner, though it does demonstrate my early tendencies toward community-minded projects.

> POOR RICHARD ONCE SAID, "THE DOORS OF WISDOM ARE NEVER SHUT."

A salt marsh lay at the edge of the mill pond near our home, and at high water we would go there to fish for minnows. Our fishing hole soon became a quagmire, so I proposed to build a pier upon which we could stand and fish. I led my friends to a large heap of stones which were intended for a new house near the marsh, but we could certainly put them to our own uses. After the workers had gone home for the day, I assembled my playmates and we worked like a bunch of little ants, sometimes two or three to a stone. Every stone meant to build the house was used instead to build our fishing pier. The removal was immediately noticed by the workers the next morning and our wrong was soon discovered. Most of us were corrected by our fathers and, in my own defense, I pleaded the usefulness of the work but to no avail. Father convinced me that nothing could be enduringly useful which was not honestly done.

CHAPTER 5

Early Employments and My Introduction to Various Trades

Speaking to you from my role as a college professor, in my opinion, Franklin's father aided his son tremendously by taking him around town and exposing him to all the various trades. If my students suffer from any deficiency, it is that they have not been exposed to a broad variety of jobs before coming to college. Parents can give their child a lifelong advantage by intentionally introducing him or her to as many kinds of work as possible. In the absence of such exposure, students will gravitate toward what they find easy or familiar, and this might not always be what's best for them or their community.

I CONTINUED WORKING IN MY FATHER'S CANDLE business for two more years until I turned 12 years old. My older brother John had been trained by my father to take over this business. However, he left the household, got married, and moved to Rhode Island. It seemed that I was destined to take his place and make

> POOR RICHARD ONCE SAID, "HE THAT HATH A TRADE, HATH AN ESTATE."

candles for the rest of my life. I disliked the smelly, repetitive work of candle-making and father knew this. He feared that I would become a sailor if he did not soon find a trade that interested me. After all, father had already had one son, my brother Josiah, go off to sea, and this annoyed him greatly.

So my father took me for walks around town from time to time. This gave me the chance to observe a variety of furniture and cabinet makers, bricklayers, craftsmen who worked with brass, and many others at their work. Father's hope was to find a trade that interested me and would keep me on land instead of at sea. Three lifelong benefits emerged from these walks together. First, I continue to enjoy watching talented craftsmen at work with their tools. Second, by observing them, I learned to do odd jobs around my own home when a handyman was not available. Finally, I've built more than a few small machines for my science experiments while the idea was fresh in my mind because I've some idea of how things work.

Ultimately, my father decided that I would learn the craft of making knives and other types of cutting tools. My uncle Benjamin's son, Samuel, had learned that business in London and had just set up shop in Boston. Father sent me over to his shop to arrange an apprenticeship and was disappointed to learn that Samuel expected a fee for teaching me the trade. As with other expensive endeavors, father once again decided it would be cheaper to keep me at home.

> Great entrepreneurs often have very humble beginnings. John D. Rockefeller's father was a peddler. Henry Ford grew up working on a farm. Former Interstate Batteries CEO Norm Miller worked in gas stations.

CHAPTER 6

First Attempts at Self-Improvement

One of Franklin's sisters noted that she recalled him reading his Bible at the young age of five—quite an accomplishment for his day. Writing would soon follow, and Franklin took the initiative to improve his mastery of both skills rather than wait for the chance of returning to school. This chapter details his earliest efforts at self-improvement, one of Franklin's quintessential characteristics. He also begins work as an apprentice in his older brother's print shop. Apprentices were little more than indentured servants, contracting with their masters in exchange for work, room, and board. After a specified period of time, an apprentice could be promoted to a wage-earning journeyman and later become master of his own shop. Along with an explanation of life as an apprentice, Franklin offers his counsel as to why arguing is ultimately a bad habit.

SINCE MY CHILDHOOD I'VE LOVED READING, and every cent that came my way I used to purchase books. I greatly admired John Bunyan's Pilgrim's Progress, and so my first purchase was a collection of his writings. I later sold Bunyan and used that money to buy R. Burton's Historical Collections—a series of 40 or so inexpensive books. Father's small library consisted primarily of books about religious disputes. I read many of them and later regretted the choice as I was no longer going to become a clergyman. Plutarch's Lives was also on his shelf, however, and I still consider my multiple readings of those volumes to be time well spent. I also had the chance to read Daniel DeFoe's Essay on Projects and also Cotton Mather's Essays to Do Good. I'll have more to say about Mather's book later on as it had a particularly significant impact on my thinking.

My father observed my love of books and reading and decided that I should become a printer, even though my brother James was already one. James had set up shop in Boston in 1717, with a press and set of types that he brought back from England. Although I still harbored dreams of going to sea, I liked the idea of being a printer far more than being a candle maker. Father lost no time getting me set up as an apprentice to my brother. I stalled in a last-ditch effort to go to sea, but eventually relented and signed an apprenticeship contract at a mere 12 years old. In effect, I was condemned to be nothing more than an indentured servant for the first eight years and then receive journeyman's wages in my last year.

I mastered the business in no time at all and became a good investment for my brother. My new work allowed me access to more and better books, as I often interacted with the apprentices to booksellers. I could now borrow books instead of buy them, and I made sure I returned them quickly and in perfect condition. Often, this meant that I stayed up reading in my room the better part of the night so that I could return the book the morning after it was borrowed, before it was missed.

A local tradesman, Matthew Adams, was a frequent customer in our print shop and soon noticed my love of reading. He was an educated man with a fine library to which he invited me and lent me any book I wished to read. This introduced me to poetry, and I started writing some of my own short pieces. Noting the new interest, my brother James asked me to compose poetic ballads every now and then that we could print and distribute for money. One of my earliest was called *The Lighthouse Tragedy,* and set to verse the sad story of the drowning of Captain Worthilake and his two daughters. Another was a sailor's song about the final battle of the pirate Blackbeard. To be honest, they were terrible poems but we printed them anyway and I went about town selling them.

The Lighthouse Tragedy sold a good number as it was both a recent and well-known tragedy. This success went to my head, and I considered becoming a poet. My father brought me back down to earth, however, by poking fun at my recitations and informing me that all the poets he knew were beggars. This discouraged me from becoming a poet and most likely a very bad one. However, I proved to have more of a knack for writing prose, as the following story will illustrate. I consider my ability to write prose to be one of the keys to my success.

I befriended another bookish fellow in town named John Collins. We loved to argue with each other and our contests began to escalate. By the way, arguing becomes a habit—a very bad habit—and because you must be contradictory to start an argument, you'll soon offend the people around you. Not only do you sour and spoil otherwise pleasant conversation, you make enemies where you should be making friends. I trace this bad habit back to the reading of my father's books about religious disputes. I now know that sensible people both avoid starting arguments and getting trapped in them. The only exceptions to this include lawyers, professors, and—as the old joke goes—hard-headed Scots.

POOR RICHARD ONCE SAID, "BY DILIGENCE AND PATIENCE, THE MOUSE BIT IN TWO THE CABLE."

Collins and I once debated the wisdom of educating women and what abilities they might have for study. He thought it improper to educate a woman, and that they could never keep up with men should they be allowed to pursue an education. I argued to the contrary to help the argument heat up. Collins had a natural eloquence and had plenty of stock rebuttals at the ready. I often found myself giving in, not to the strength of his reasoning, but to the fluency with which his ideas were presented to me. We parted without settling the matter, and I decided to write down my arguments and send them by mail since we were not to see one another again for some time. He answered my letters, I replied to his, and we kept our debate going for many months. Father found these letters, read through them, and decided to coach me to improve my writing. He started with the positives: I was better than Collins in both spelling and punctuation given my work in the print shop. Unfortunately, he showed me several examples where my shortcomings in eloquence, structure, and clarity were causing my opponent to get the better of me. I concluded that his feedback was correct and decided to put myself on a program to improve my writing. Here's how I did it.

I purchased a collection of *Spectator* magazines, a popular publication about philosophy, politics, and literature. I read them cover to cover several times and found the writing to be everything mine was not. The challenge now was to bring my writing up to these standards. I briefly outlined several of the articles published in the *Spectator* and then set them aside for a few days. Then, working only from my brief outline and not looking at the book, I tried to write out each of the papers again. My goal was for my reconstruction to capture the logic and emotion of the original documents. I would then compare my reconstruction with the original article, pinpoint my faults, and correct them.

I realized the need to improve my vocabulary and turned back to poetry as an aid in this endeavor. Poetry demands that the writer master a variety of words and phrases that capture the primary meaning but come at it from different directions. Who knows? Maybe my previous poetic musings were not wasted effort after all. I took some of the literary stories from the *Spectator* and transformed them into poetic verse. Then, just as I did with the position papers, I laid them aside for a time and then tried to reconstruct the prose from my own poetry. Another self-improvement exercise I developed was to jumble my outlines of the position papers and—after several weeks had passed—try to reconstruct the outlines into the proper order again. This exercise taught me how to structure my thoughts in the proper order before writing all the sentences.

These exercises vastly improved my writing abilities. Furthermore, I sometimes imagined—true or not—that I improved a few of the articles and stories in some minor places. Such successes gave me confidence that I might one day write things that others would want to read not once but many times over. This became my obsession. I did these writing exercises in the morning before work began and in the evening, when it had ended. I still thought church attendance a duty but could not justify going on Sundays given the improvements I was making in my own writing by working alone in the quiet of the print shop.

> Great businesspeople are almost always great readers. Gary Heavin, founder of the Curves franchise, describes himself as an avid reader who reads one book each week. Twice each year, Bill Gates leaves Microsoft for a weeklong reading retreat he calls "Think Week."

CHAPTER 7

Experimenting with Vegetarianism

We fancy that we invented vegetarianism in the latter third of the 20th century. Rather, vegetarianism was alive and well in the 18th century, and Franklin decided to give it a try very early in his life. He undertook the endeavor because of the money he could save, but it also shows us his fondness for experimentation. This tendency would one day win him international acclaim as a scientist.

WHEN I WAS ABOUT 16 YEARS OLD I CAME across Thomas Tryon's book, *The Way to Health, Wealth, and Happiness*, which recommended a vegetable diet. I liked what I read and determined to start experimenting with his ideas in my life. My brother was responsible for my food and lodging since I was his apprentice. He had neither house nor wife so he rented rooms for himself and his apprentices from another family. My decision to begin a vegetable diet soon caused a great deal of trouble at the dinner table, and my brother scolded me for being so peculiar.

It wasn't hard to prepare Tryon's recommended vegetable dishes. Even a 16-year-old can boil potatoes and rice or make a few simple casseroles. So I made a

> POOR RICHARD ONCE SAID, "TO LENGTHEN THY LIFE, LESSEN THY MEALS."

deal with my brother: if he would each week give me the money he paid others to feed me, I would use that money to feed myself. He jumped at the deal, most likely because of the embarrassment I caused him at meal times. I quickly discovered that I could feed myself on half of what he paid others to feed me. I used the other half of the funds to buy more books.

Another personal advantage emerged from this diet. My brother and the other apprentices would leave the print shop to go to their meals, leaving me there alone. My lighter meals took no time at all to eat and I could use their time away from the shop to continue my studies and self-improvement exercises. From this I learned that great benefits accompany eating in moderation and drinking water instead of alcohol with meals. The quietness of the shop combined with the vigor of the diet gave a focus and retention to my learning that I had never enjoyed before.

The inventor of cornflakes, W.K. Kellogg, was also a vegetarian. More recently, Whole Foods Market founder John Mackey and Apple Computer founder Steve Jobs have enjoyed this lifestyle.

CHAPTER 8

Where We Learned "Win Friends and Influence People"

Self-improvement guru Dale Carnegie praised Franklin's autobiography as "one of the most fascinating life stories ever written and one of the classics of American literature." Franklin graces numerous pages in Carnegie's classic book How to Win Friends and Influence People. *Reading this chapter, it's easy to see why. Observe how Franklin draws out great interpersonal skills from classic sources. For him, all education was self-education. Though he enjoyed a few years of formal schooling, he taught himself most of the really valuable skills.*

DURING THIS TIME I DECIDED TO OVERCOME MY earlier failures in mathematics. I picked up an arithmetic text and found, much to my pleasure, that I could easily master the exercises it contained. I also read some books about marine navigation and began to acquaint myself with the realm of geometry (although I would never proceed far in that science). At this age I also first read Locke's *On Human Understanding* and du Port Royal's book on the *Art of Thinking*.

Wanting to develop my vocabulary even further, I read an English grammar textbook. At the back of the book, there were some good examples of rhetoric and logic, one of which was part of a Socratic dialogue. Eager to learn more about his methods, I obtained a copy of Xenophon's book *Memorable Things of Socrates* as it contained a variety of Socratic dialogues. His example convinced me to drop my habits of immediately contradicting other people and pushing hard for my opinions. Rather, I stopped arguing my side and starting asking questions instead.

Another book had convinced me of the wisdom of speaking from a stance of curiosity rather than certainty—especially in matters of religious doctrine. I soon found these methods both kept me from a great deal of embarrassment and frustrated anyone who tried to argue with me. I couldn't help but love the results and I practiced my new skills whenever I could. As a result, I became an expert at gaining concessions from people more knowledgeable in the subject at hand. Even from a weaker position, I gained victories by either leading my opponents to the point of contradiction or toward unsavory consequences of their ideas which they did not foresee.

> POOR RICHARD ONCE SAID, "WOULD YOU PERSUADE, SPEAK OF INTEREST, NOT OF REASON."

I stayed with the method only a few years, so I can't give it a complete endorsement. Yet I do retain one good habit: I express my position humbly rather than forcefully. When I speak on matters even the least bit controversial, I still avoid the words "certainly," "undoubtedly," or any other that might give the air of certainty to my opinions. Rather, I say, "It's my perception that . . ." or "Given the information that I have . . ." or "Correct me if I'm wrong . . ."

I have found these conversational habits most useful when I've had to influence others to my point of view to get something done. I hope the reasonable, well-intentioned people who read this book will stop arguing in hopes of getting their way. Arguing only makes enemies—angry enemies at that—and undermines the very purpose of civil discourse, which is the giving and receiving of information, pleasantly or persuasively. Arguing creates immediate defensiveness and prevents the other party from even hearing your side of the matter. You simply cannot change the mind of others and at the same time show no desire to change your own mind. Wiser people—who know that arguing is a waste of time—will probably listen courteously and then leave you in

Stephen Covey's book *The 7 Habits of Highly Effective People* presents Franklin as the personification of the "Character Ethic." The ethic contends that internal character, rather than external facade, is the foundation of success.

possession of your error rather than take time to educate you when you've already proven yourself a fool. In the end, arguing neither pleases nor persuades anyone.

Wise counsel is contained in the old saying:

Men should be taught as if you taught them not,
And things unknown proposed as things forgot.

CHAPTER 9

The Yearning for Independence

Throughout the course of his life, Franklin found it convenient to convey his ideas through an assumed name and identity rather than his own. "Poor" Richard Saunders and Miss Polly Baker are among his best-known alternate personalities. Some scholars even argue that the Benjamin Franklin we read about in the autobiography is his most masterful creation. Franklin creates his first alter ego in this chapter—a sharp-tongued widow named Silence Dogood. Franklin wrote a number of essays under this pseudonym and they were published in his brother's newspaper to great acclaim. The new identity could not shield Franklin from the realities of his life, however. His description of the deteriorating relationship with his brother is a warning to harsh supervisors everywhere of the long-lived impact of bad management.

IN 1721, MY BROTHER JAMES BEGAN TO PRINT a newspaper named the *New England Courant.* It was the second paper to be printed in America, preceded only by the *Boston Newsletter.* Some of his friends tried to talk him out of printing the paper as they were convinced that there was not enough market share for two newspapers in America. As I write these 50 years later, America has no fewer than 25 papers. Thankfully, James went against the advice of his friends and printed the paper anyway. I was employed setting the type, printing off the sheets, and carrying the papers through the streets to subscribers and customers.

Some of his educated friends started writing for the paper. Their contributions boosted the reputation of the paper and demand began to grow. They often visited the print shop. This gave me a chance to listen to their conversations, which always included a hearty round of self-congratulations. I decided that this paper was the perfect venue for my newly developed writing skills, but I faced a couple of problems. First, they considered me a mere boy—and I was. Second, I knew my brother well enough to know that he would never print anything in his paper if he knew it was mine. Therefore, the situation called for a different strategy.

I disguised my handwriting, wrote an anonymous paper, and slipped it under the door of the print shop one night. The next morning it was found on the floor and brought to the regular meeting of James and his writing friends. They read it and, as I went about my work in the shop, they commented on it in my hearing. I had the exquisite pleasure of hearing that the writing met with their approval. Better still, as they tried to guess the identity of the anonymous author, the names they mentioned were educated men of greater intelligence than mine. Looking back on it now, however, I was lucky to have had judges whose editorial discernment I had overestimated at the time.

> POOR RICHARD ONCE SAID, "IF YOU RIDE A HORSE, SIT CLOSE AND TIGHT, IF YOU RIDE A MAN, SIT EASY AND LIGHT."

Nonetheless, I was considerably lifted by the entire episode. I wrote and delivered several more papers anonymously and they were all approved for publication. I managed to keep the scheme going for some time. My need for approval was too strong to keep my identity secret for very long, though, and I ultimately revealed myself to my brother's friends. Their admiration for me grew after my revelation, but not so with my brother. Rather, he thought the whole incident had made me arrogant, and I'm sure I gave him little evidence to the contrary.

This is probably where he and I started having real difficulties in our relationship. He was my brother, but he also considered himself my master. As a result, he expected the same services of me as he would of any other apprentice. I expected better treatment from family and found much of the work he had me do more demeaning than necessary. We fought often and asked father to arbitrate our disputes. His judgments were generally in my favor so either I was in the right more often than not, or just knew how to frame my case better than my brother. My brother would take out his frustrations by beating me, sometimes rather severely. These beatings made me despise both my brother and my apprenticeship, and I began thinking about ways to break my contract rather than continue to endure such treatment. One good thing came of these experiences, however. They gave me a loathing for tyranny and oppression that even now, as I write this in 1771, grows in importance with each passing year.

CHAPTER 10

Breaking Loose to Freedom

A Founding Father, Franklin was influential in winning freedom of the press for the United States. Most likely this is because Franklin understood firsthand the dangers the media faced when the press lacked protection. Franklin teaches us here that change is often a dangerous opportunity. That is, dangers often present us with unexpected opportunities. In running away from his brother, Franklin may have been right or may have been wrong; but he certainly wasn't indecisive.

BEFORE TOO LONG ONE OF OUR POLITICAL WRITINGS offended the Assembly. My brother James was arrested, publicly denounced, and imprisoned for a month because he wouldn't name the author of the piece. I was also cross-examined before the council. Since I was only an apprentice, however, they gave me a stern warning and dismissed me, assuming that I'd keep my master's secrets—which I did. Despite the friction in our relationship, I thought my brother's imprisonment to be quite unjust. Nonetheless, it gave me the management of the paper during his time in jail, and I determined to use the opportunity to strike back

> POOR RICHARD ONCE SAID, "HE'S A FOOL THAT MAKES HIS DOCTOR HIS HEIR."

at the ruling authorities. My brother appreciated the favor, but others viewed me as a promising citizen on the slippery slope to libel and satire.

My brother's imprisonment was accompanied by a very strange order from the Assembly. It read, "James Franklin should no longer print the paper called the *New England Courant*." All of us involved in the newspaper gathered at the print shop to decide how we should respond. One suggestion was to print the paper under a new title. James disliked this idea, however, as he had worked hard and suffered much to establish the name of the paper. We ultimately decided to print the paper using the name of "Benjamin Franklin" as the publisher. To prevent the Assembly from accusing him of printing the paper under the name of his apprentice, my papers of indenture were returned to me with a fake but full discharge written on the back in my brother's hand. I could show these to the Assembly should the accusation arise that I was still his apprentice. These were only for show, however. In reality, I was forced to sign new papers of indenture for the remainder of my service, to be held by my brother in private. Admittedly, it was the flimsiest of schemes, but a new paper came out almost immediately under my name and we continued to publish for several months.

Once James was released from jail and the trouble passed, he and I resumed our previous disagreements. Believing that things would not improve, I took the opportunity to break free of my brother's indenture, assuming James too cowardly to call me on the fake contract we created. This was opportunistic, I admit, and I still consider it the first big mistake of my life. Truth be known, however, the unfairness of the act weighed little on my conscience, given all the beatings he gave me. James was not a bad man; he just beat me when he became angry . . . and I was probably too provoking.

Great entrepreneurs have always benefited from tough life experiences. Our competitors often force us to levels we would not have reached on our own. Where would Steve Jobs and Apple computer be without Bill Gates, and vice versa?

CHAPTER 11

Testing My Determination

Franklin decides to run away to New York City to seek his fortune, like so many teenagers since. In those days, however, even paying customers were asked by coachmen and captains their business for traveling, and you could be fined for helping someone who broke an indenture. Franklin proved his mettle immediately with what turned out to be a very difficult journey between his home in Boston and his new home in Philadelphia. Along the way, Franklin shares with us a humorous story about his falling away from his vegetarian diet. The story illuminates his love of reason for resolving conflicts with either oneself or another, and ends with a classic line from the always quotable Franklin.

JAMES DID NOT LET ME GO EASILY, HOWEVER. After I broke my indentures, he talked with the master of every other print shop in town, cautioning them not to hire me. Nobody in Boston would hire me now, so I decided to go to the nearest town large enough to support a printing trade: New York City. My writing had already offended the governing party and—given the sort of "justice" that attended by brother's problem with the Assembly—there was a good chance that I could end up in jail, or worse, given my situation. Further, Boston is just not the place to raise questions about religion as I had done in some of my writings. Some of the Puritans already pointed at me in horror, considering me an infidel or atheist. Finally, my father sided with James as to the injustice of my leaving my apprenticeship. I could not make a new life for myself in this city under these circumstances. It was best to leave.

My friend Collins stepped in to help me at this point. He negotiated my passage with the captain of a ship bound for New York City. He told the captain that I was a friend of his who had got a girl pregnant and that her family would force me to marry her were I to be seen in public. I sold some of my books to pay for my passage and was taken aboard the ship very covertly.

Before I tell about my arrival in New York City, allow me the chance to share a humorous event that happened along the way. Owing to a lack of wind, our ship dropped anchor off Block Island. The passengers and crew began fishing to catch cod and hauled in a large catch. At this point in my life, I had enjoyed a vegetarian diet for about 18 months. After reading Tryon's aforementioned book, I became convinced that eating fish or any other meat was nothing less than cold-blooded murder, since none of the animals we slaughter had or ever could harm us so severely as to deserve death. For the past year and a half, all of this had seemed very reasonable to me.

Previously, I had greatly enjoyed dining on fish and when those cod came hot out of the frying pan that day, they smelled wonderful. I struggled mightily between my dietary principles and the present temptation. I then recalled that when the cod were opened and cleaned, the cooks removed smaller fish out of the cods' own stomachs. So I thought to myself, "If fish can eat one another, why can't we eat fish?" As a result, I have rarely enjoyed a more pleasing and hearty serving of cod than I did that day in the company of my fellow passengers, and I have since returned to a vegetarian diet only occasionally. It's so useful to be a reasonable creature, since it enables one either to find or to make a reason for everything one would like to do.

Back to the voyage. Finally, a fair wind arose and three days after leaving Boston I found myself 300 miles from home, in New York City. Here I was, a 17-year-old boy in a strange city with no friends or acquaintances, no letter to recommend me as a person of good character, and almost no money in my pocket. Most boys in my situation would have gone to sea, but I no longer cared for the seafaring life since I now had a trade. I was confident in my talent and work ethic, though, so I went to the only print shop in New York City. It was owned by a fellow named William Bradford. He had too little business and too many hands to offer me employment, but he did offer some valuable information. "My son in Philadelphia had his best worker, a fellow named Aquila Rose, die on him suddenly," Bradford informed me. "If you go there quickly, I believe he may have room to employ someone like you."

Philadelphia was a hundred more miles away, and I would have to get there quickly if I were to capitalize on this opportunity. I set out immediately in a boat for Amboy, leaving my chest with my personal belongings to follow by sea in a bigger ship. As we crossed the bay in our small boat, a very high wind tore our rotten sails to pieces and prevented our reaching the Kill Van Kull waters—the easiest passage to our destination. Instead, the wind drove us in the opposite direction toward Long Island. It was a wretched trip with only one positive memory, which I'll relate to you now.

As we sailed, a drunken Dutchman on the boat fell overboard and sank quickly. I pulled him by his hair from under the water before he drowned, and we got him into the boat again. His dunking sobered him a bit and he decided he would sleep. Before he lay down, however, he took a book out of his pocket and asked if I would dry it out for him. I was pleased to learn that the book was my old favorite, *Pilgrim's Progress,* by John Bunyan. In was printed in Dutch on fine paper with handsome engravings—a better package than any English version I had yet seen. I've since learned that the book has been translated into most of the languages of Europe, making it probably the most widely read book except for the Bible. I think the key to Bunyan's success was that he was the first to mix narration and dialogue, whereas much of what preceded him was either all narration or all dialogue, like the Socratic dialogues. His innovation brought the reader into the story in ways that no other writer managed to do before him. Daniel Defoe imitated this method in his books *Robinson Crusoe*, *Moll Flanders*, and others with great success, as did Samuel Richardson in his book *Pamela*.

Here's the rest of the story about that terrible trip. The wind drove us over to Long Island, toward a place with a rocky beach and high surf. There was no way our boat could land there so we dropped anchor and waited for the wind to die down. Some locals came down to the shore and called to us and we tried to respond. The wind was so strong and the surf so loud that we could not communicate with one another. There were some canoes on shore, and we signaled to them to use them to come fetch us. They either didn't understand us or thought it too dangerous so they went away. Night was coming and our situation was dire. We had no choice but to wait for the wind to die down.

The boatman and I decided to sleep if we could so we crowded into the small covered area that already held the still-drenched Dutchman. The high wind drove the spray from the sea over our boat, and it leaked down upon us through the cracks, and soon the boat contained three drenched passengers. We made the night like this, sleeping very little. Thankfully, the wind died down the next day, and we were able to reach Amboy without spending a second night on the water. In all, we spent thirty hours on the ocean without any food and only a bottle of filthy rum to drink.

In the evening when we landed, I had a high fever and decided it was best to go to bed. I had read that one could break a fever by drinking plenty of cold water. I followed that prescription, sweated heavily most of the night, and my fever had left me by morning. The next day I crossed the Raritan River by ferry and continued my journey on foot. My destination was Burlington, where I could find a boat on the Delaware River to carry me the rest of the way to Philadelphia.

It rained hard all the next day and I was thoroughly soaked. By noon, I was tired of walking and stopped at a cheap inn, where I spent the night. I had now begun to wish that I had never left home. Obviously, I looked horrible and I could tell by the questions people asked me that I was assumed to be a

> POOR RICHARD ONCE SAID, "YOU MAY DELAY, BUT TIME WILL NOT."

runaway servant. I began to fear being arrested on that suspicion. I moved on the next day, walked through to the evening, and made it to within eight to ten miles of Burlington. I stayed at an inn kept by a Dr. Brown. He began talking with me as I ate and became very sociable when he learned I was somewhat well-read. He knew a great deal about seemingly every town in England and every country in Europe. From this I assumed that he was a traveling doctor in his day. He was quite intelligent, college-educated, and a relentless unbeliever. Our friendship continued as long as he lived, and he sent me some occasional writings. Many years after my visit, he wrote a parody of the Bible making many of its claims look quite ridiculous. Had he ever published the work, he might have succeeded in injuring some of the weaker minds in the world.

After a good night's sleep, I continued my journey to Burlington and reached it late the next morning. To my great disappointment, the boats had sailed for Philadelphia just a few hours before my arrival and no more were expected to sail to Philadelphia for three more days. I had purchased some gingerbread for my presumed voyage from an older woman in town, and I returned to her to seek some advice. She had no advice but invited me to stay at her house until the boats sailed in a few days. I was tired of walking and accepted her invitation. When she learned I was a printer she suggested that I stay in Burlington and start printing immediately. Although naïve to the difficulties of starting and maintaining a print shop, she was an otherwise good host who fed me a dinner of ox cheek, accepting only a pot of ale in return. I left the house thinking it a good place to stay a few days as I headed to the riverside for an evening stroll.

Much to my surprise, a boat came down the Delaware heading for Philadelphia. The people on board agreed to take me in and we rowed all the way down the river as there was no wind. About midnight, some of the people began to think that we had rowed right past Philadelphia in the darkness and they refused to row further. No one could say quite where we were so we left the river, went a bit up a creek, and went ashore. Being October, it was a cold night and we made a fire out of an old fence near which we landed. Once the sun was up, one of our company recognized our location as Cooper's Creek, a little north of Philadelphia. We returned to the river and rowed to Philadelphia in no time at all. We landed at the Market Street wharf early Sunday morning.

CHAPTER 12

My Unlikely Beginning in Philadelphia

Franklin is everywhere in Philadelphia. The vast majority of the city's more than 40 public sculptures of Franklin celebrate the mature man at the peak of his powers. Yet few people who have ascended to dominate the global stage—and lived to write about it—started off worse than he. Franklin provides us this unflattering portrait of his arrival in his new hometown. Maybe one of Franklin's greatest legacies is that he showed us that we can finish better than our beginnings.

I'LL NOW SHARE MORE DETAILS WITH YOU ABOUT my first day in Philadelphia so that you may fully appreciate the difference between where I started and who I have now become. My good clothes were still coming around from New York by sea. Thus, I began my life in Philadelphia in my working clothes. I was filthy from my journey. Every pocket on my person was stuffed with some shirt or stocking. Worse yet, I knew no one, nor where to look for lodging. The boat trip down the Delaware had exhausted me with all the rowing and the lack of sleep. And I was very hungry, too. The only cash I had left consisted of one Dutch dollar and a shilling in copper. I gave the copper to the owners of the boat to pay for my passage. They refused it, saying that I had rowed too much to be a paying passenger, but I insisted that they take it. You know, a man is sometimes more generous when he's almost broke than when he has plenty of money, probably for fear of being thought poor.

I walked a good way up the street observing all the activity, and I met a boy with some bread. I asked him where he got it, as I had made many a meal on bread, and I followed his directions immediately to the baker on Second Street. Knowing only to ask for what we had in Boston, I asked for a biscuit, but they didn't make such in Philadelphia. I then asked for another common Boston bread, the three-penny loaf, but was again told they had no such thing. Having no clue as to the differences in money, the makes of bread, nor the best value for my money, I gave the baker three pennies' worth of my money and asked for bread. In return, he gave me three large puffy rolls. I was surprised at the quantity but took them anyway. Having no room left in my pockets, I walked off with one roll under each arm while eating the third.

> POOR RICHARD ONCE SAID, "HE IS ILL-CLOTH'D WHO IS BARE OF VIRTUE."

Thus I went up Market Street as far as Fourth Street, passing by the home of the Read family where my future wife, Deborah, lived. She stood at the door as I passed by and her expression suggested to me that I must have looked pretty ridiculous—an assessment with which I could not disagree. I turned down Chestnut Street and part of Walnut Street, eating my roll all the way. Ultimately, I came back around to the place on the Market Street wharf where I first arrived and took a good drink from the river. My stomach now filled by one of the rolls, I gave the other two to a woman and her child who had come down the river in the boat with us and were waiting to go farther.

Feeling refreshed, I walked back up the street and found a crowd of neatly dressed people all walking in the same direction. I followed them closely and ended up in the great Quaker meeting house near the market. I sat down among them, waiting for something to happen but it stayed quiet. My lack of sleep caught up with me as I sat there and I fell fast asleep. Apparently, I slept through the entire gathering and one of the Quakers was kind enough to wake me up as everyone began to disperse. Thus, the Quakers were the first to extend me hospitality when I arrived in Philadelphia.

CHAPTER 13

My First Job

Franklin benefited from both good sense and good timing after he left home. He wisely chose to rest and refresh himself before seeking work. His ability to make a good impression, coupled with a bit of good fortune, results in his landing his first job in Philadelphia. Along the way, he realizes the competitive danger of talking too loosely to strangers.

THE MEETING NOW OVER, I LEFT THE BUILDING and walked back down toward the river. I found a kind-looking young Quaker and asked him whether he could tell me where someone new to Philadelphia might find lodging. We were standing near the Three Mariners Inn and he said, "A newcomer could lodge here but it doesn't have a good reputation. If you're willing to walk with me a bit, I'll take you to a better place." He brought me to the Crooked Billet on Water Street, where I ate my first good meal in several days. As I ate, my hosts carefully questioned me as they seemed to suspect from both my youth and appearance that I was a runaway.

After lunch I decided to sleep a bit. I lay down on the bed without undressing and slept until six that evening. I awoke when called to dinner but went to bed again after eating and slept soundly until the next morning. I cleaned up as best I could and went off the find Andrew Bradford's print shop. I found the shop and was surprised to discover in the shop his father William, the older man I met in New York who recommended I come this way. He had traveled on horse-back and had arrived in Philadelphia before me. He remembered me and intro-duced me to his son who received me very civilly, giving me a breakfast. Unfortunately, he did not need any help at present as he had just brought in a new worker. However, he knew of a printer who had just set up shop in town—a fellow named Keimer—and he might employ me. If not, Bradford offered to lodge me at his home and give me a bit of work now and then in his print shop until I could find full-time employment.

The elder Bradford accompanied me to the other print shop. "Neighbor," Bradford said to Keimer, "I have with me a young man who knows the printing business. Perhaps you might be in need of one." Keimer asked me a few ques-tions, tested my skills with a composing stick, and claimed that he would employ me as soon as he had enough work to support me. The two had never met before and Keimer assumed Bradford to be a well-intentioned local. He seized the opportunity to impress Bradford with talk of his business and proj-ects. Keimer boasted that he soon expected to be the dominant printer in Philadelphia, and Bradford—keeping silent about his identity—played curious and began to ask numerous questions. Eager to convince the stranger, Keimer divulged much about his strategy and clientele. This episode taught me that Bradford was a crafty businessman and Keimer a mere novice. Once Bradford left and it was my place to speak, Keimer was shocked to discover the true iden-tity of his assumed patron.

POOR RICHARD ONCE SAID, "FOOLS MAKE FEASTS AND WISE MEN EAT 'EM."

Keimer's shop was in poor shape. His printing press was ancient and his only set of fonts was worn out. Keimer's first project was composing an elegy for Andrew Bradford's for-mer hand, Aquila Rose, who had died unexpectedly. Rose, a clerk of the Assembly, was much respected in town and known to be both intel-ligent and a good poet. Keimer, quite frankly, seemed to be neither. Rather than write down his verse, he composed it in his head and set it directly to type. There being no copy and only one set of type for what appeared to be a lengthy elegy, there was no way I could help. Thus, I hoped to make myself useful by getting his printing press in working order. He had not yet used it nor did it appear he knew how it worked. This I did and promised to return to help him print off his elegy once it was complete. I departed for Bradford's to lodge and eat, and was pleased to find a small job at his place to keep me busy. Keimer sent for me in a few days, to come help print off the elegy. During that time, he had purchased another set of fonts. He put me to work setting a pamphlet order which he had taken in my absence.

What little experience I had in my brother's shop told me that neither of these printers were qualified for the business. Bradford was illiterate and, though the son of a printer, had spent no time whatsoever learning the business in his youth. A bit more learned, Keimer was a poor writer and knew nothing about how to work the press. He had been a member of a radical French religious sect but seemed now to practice a bit of every religion. He was ignorant about the workings of the world and, as I would soon discover, somewhat of a scoundrel.

Keimer did not like my lodging at Bradford's while I worked with him and set about to change that. He had a house but no furniture, so he could not lodge me himself. So he lodged me with the aforementioned Read family. My chest and clothes had arrived from New York by this time, allowing me to make a more respectable impression on their daughter, who had first seen me eating my roll as I walked along the street.

First jobs can lead to great things. McDonald's, often the target of "McJob" jokes, trains more young people than the American armed forces. Former CEO Jim Cantalupo contended that "McJob" should be defined as "teaches responsibility" instead of more derogatory characterizations.

CHAPTER 14

Big Promises from a Fancy Politician

In the last chapter, Franklin showed us his wisdom in knowing how to make a good impression. In this one, he reminds us that he's as susceptible to folly as any youth (though it will take us a few chapters to finish the story). Nevertheless, it seems clear to everybody in the area that this young Franklin is a talented fellow.

MY LIFE IN PHILADELPHIA BEGAN TO IMPROVE, and I slowly forgot my old life in Boston. I began to make friends with some young people in Philadelphia who were lovers of reading. My evenings were made more pleasant by this company. I worked hard and saved most of my money. Only one person knew my whereabouts—my friend John Collins—and he was sworn to secrecy, given that I was a runaway. Nonetheless, something happened that sent me back to Boston sooner than I had intended.

I had a brother-in-law, Robert Holmes, who was captain of a small ship that traded between Boston and Delaware. While stopped at New Castle, 40 miles south of Philadelphia, he heard about me. He wrote me a letter about how concerned everyone in Boston was about my abrupt departure. He assured me that nothing bad would happen to me should I decide to return, and he encouraged me to do so. I answered his letter and thanked him for his advice. I also took the opportunity to give him a full account of my reasons for leaving Boston. Knowing the news would travel beyond him, I framed my case as convincingly as possible.

The provincial governor of Pennsylvania, Sir William Keith, resided in New Castle, Delaware, at the time. Captain Holmes just happened to be with him when my letter arrived. He spoke to the governor about me and showed him the letter. He read it and was surprised to find out that I was only a teenager. Having a low regard for the two current printers and a high regard for my talents, he proclaimed that I should set up my own shop in Philadelphia. My success was virtually inevitable as he would choose me to print the government's business and aid me in every other way. All of this my brother-in-law told me later. I knew nothing of it when the story I'm about to tell you happened.

Not long after the exchange of letters, Keimer and I were working together near the window of the print shop when we saw the governor coming our way. He was accompanied by another gentleman from New Castle, Colonel French, and they were finely dressed. As they arrived at the door of the shop, Keimer quickly ran down, thrilled that the governor had come to visit him. Much to our surprise, the governor asked for me. With a politeness between ages and classes I had not yet experienced, he profusely complimented me, expressed a desire to become better acquainted, kindly chastised me for not making myself known to him when I first arrived in Philadelphia, and asked me to join him and the colonel at the tavern to enjoy some excellent Madeira wine. Through the entire conversation, Keimer could only stare from the sidelines in utter disbelief.

> POOR RICHARD ONCE SAID, "THE FAVOR OF THE GREAT IS NO INHERITANCE."

We went off to the tavern on the corner of Third Street, and over the Madeira he suggested I set up my own business. He outlined the competitive landscape for me and both he and Colonel French assured me that they would work to procure for me the public business of both the Pennsylvania and Delaware governments. When I suggested that my father would have doubts about assisting me in such an endeavor, Sir William pledged to write a letter of recommendation to which my father couldn't help but agree. We concluded that I should return to

Boston on the first possible vessel carrying the governor's letter of recommendation. In the meantime, the plan would be kept secret, and I would continue to work for Keimer. Every so often, Sir William would send for me to join him at dinner, and he chatted with me like a long-lost friend as we ate together. At the time, I thought it a great honor.

CHAPTER 15

Returning Home to Boston

Franklin returns to Boston and works to mend relations with his parents. He had left Boston the first time without their blessing, and he would not make the same mistake a second time. He hopes to do the same with his brother, but makes less progress. Nonetheless, he must be credited for his willingness to try to reconcile with the people he had wronged. Though we can't go through life without disappointing or even hurting others, we lessen the impact when we take the initiative to make things right again.

NOT LONG AFTER THESE EVENTS, A SHIP sailed for Boston and I took a leave of absence from Keimer, saying I was off to visit some friends. The governor sent a wonderful letter along with me addressed to my father. In the letter, Sir William complimented my many talents and assured my father that setting up my own print shop in Philadelphia was my ticket to success. Once again, the trip to Boston proved more difficult than necessary as we struck a shoal as we left the bay and sprung a leak. I took my turn pumping along with the rest as we sailed.

Despite strong winds buffeting our boat throughout the trip, we arrived safe in Boston after about two weeks on the water.

I had been gone from Boston for seven months and neither friends nor family knew anything of my condition as my brother-in-law, Captain Holmes, was yet to get word to them. As such, the visit took my family by surprise. Everyone was thrilled to see me and I was warmly welcomed by all—except, of course, my brother James. I decided to visit him at his print shop. I wore a handsome new suit and looked many times better than I did when I worked for him. I also had a new watch and a good deal of money in my pockets. He greeted me coolly, looked me over, and turned back again to his work.

His workers proved more curious and asked me for my story. I shared with them the good news about my new life in Philadelphia, expressing also my strong intention to return there. One of them asked what sort of money was in Philadelphia as Boston had a paper currency. I produced a handful of silver from my pocket and they were amazed by both the glitter and the amount. I continued my performance by showing them my watch and, as a finale, gave them some silver for a round of drinks after work. My brother sat grim and sullen through the whole show.

> POOR RICHARD ONCE SAID, "IN SUCCESS BE MODERATE."

I learned later from my mother that my visit to his shop had greatly offended him. Mother encouraged him to put the past behind him and reconcile with his younger brother. He refused and claimed that I had insulted him so much that day—and in the presence of his workers—that he could neither forgive nor forget the injury. We would both learn much later, however, that he had overestimated his ability to carry a grudge.

The governor's letter greatly surprised my father and he gave no comment on it for several days. Captain Holmes returned to Boston during this time and father asked him to read the letter, too. Father asked him his opinion of Sir William, adding that he was not impressed with a man who was so enthusiastic about setting a mere boy up in business. I was only eighteen and would not be considered a man for three more years. Holmes gave the endeavor his best recommendation, but father's opposition to the idea became apparent and, at last, he flatly refused to give his permission. Father then wrote a very nice letter back to the governor thanking him for his support and enthusiasm but declining his recommendation to set me up in business. It was his opinion that I was too young and the start-up costs were too great.

My good friend John Collins was a clerk at the post office at this time. He was so impressed with the story of my rising that he decided to join me in Philadelphia. He set out by land to Rhode Island as I was waiting for my father to make a decision about the governor's letter. He left his books, a nice collection of mathematics and natural philosophy, in my care. I would bring them along with mine to New York, where we would rendezvous.

Although my father did not approve of Sir William's proposal, he was impressed that I could obtain a strong recommendation from such a high official. It was clear that I had managed myself and my money well since I had left Boston. He saw no prospect at present for any reconciliation between my brother and me and so advised me to continue with my new life. He counseled me to behave myself in Philadelphia so that my already good reputation might continue to grow. He warned me that my continued flirting with libel and lampooning would not aid me in this effort. If I continued to work hard and manage my money conservatively, he believed I might be able to save enough money by the time I turned 21 to set up my own business. And if I needed a bit of money at that point, he would help me out then. Thus I embarked once again for Philadelphia with this good advice, some small gifts, and the blessing and approval of my parents.

———⊲◦⊳———

CHAPTER 16

More Mistakes and Bigger Promises

By this time, Franklin had learned the benefit of a good reputation. In fact, much of his father's counsel as he departed centered around keeping his reputation intact. In this chapter, he narrowly escapes serious damage to his reputation and realizes how easily that can happen to a boy who doesn't heed the counsel of his seniors. Along the way, he watches his friend fall into ruin, owing to a lack of self-discipline, and Franklin puts his own financial well-being at risk in trying to help his friend recover. Maybe Franklin's father was right, after all.

I SAILED FOR PHILADELPHIA FROM NEWPORT, Rhode Island. Before leaving, I visited my brother John, who had married and settled there years before. Our relationship was a good one and he received me very warmly. A friend of his named Vernon needed to collect 35 pounds from someone in Pennsylvania—a considerable sum. Would I be willing to collect the funds and keep them until further instructed? I agreed, and he sent me away with a written collection order. This favor would cause me a great deal of personal misery.

My ship sailed from Newport for New York with a number of interesting passengers. Among them were two young women traveling together and a serious but sensible Quaker woman traveling with attendants. Showing this woman a number of small courtesies as the voyage began, I grew in her favor. I also took the opportunity to make friends with the other two women and they, too, began to return the courtesies. Soon, the Quaker woman took me aside and said, "Young man, I am concerned for you. You clearly have no friends with you on this voyage and no idea about the ways of the world or the snares of youth. Mark my words: Those two young ladies are not to be trusted. I've been watching them closely and if you're not on your guard, they will draw you into some kind of serious trouble. You know nothing about them and not much more about me. Nonetheless, allow me this piece of well-intentioned advice: Have nothing to do with them.

I thought her judgment a bit harsh and took the occasion to question it somewhat. In response, she mentioned some things she had both observed and heard that I had not. Ultimately, she convinced me. I thanked her for her advice and promised to follow it. When we arrived in New York, these two young ladies invited me to visit them at home. I avoided the invitation and was glad I did as the next day the captain of the ship realized that a silver spoon and some other valuables had been taken from his cabin. Knowing these two girls to be prostitutes, he had their home searched, found the stolen goods, and they were arrested. So, though we had scraped a rock during our time at sea but not sank, I thought this to be the more important of the two escapes.

Once in New York, I found my friend Collins. He was extremely gifted in mathematics and, being from a privileged family, had since childhood been able to devote much of his time to studying rather than working. During my time in Boston he had lived his life well. He was widely respected, was sober and diligent in his duties, and appeared to have a wonderful future ahead of him. Once I left, however, he began to drink regularly and heavily. I was soon to learn from both him and others that he had been drunk every day since his arrival ahead of me in New York. Even worse, he had gambled while in New York and lost all his money. As a result, I had to pay his lodging there and also his traveling and living expenses in Philadelphia. All of this proved extremely inconvenient to me.

Before we left New York, the provincial governor, William Burnet, heard from the captain of our vessel that one of his passengers was a learned man who traveled with a large number of books. He called me to see him and I would have taken Collins had he been sober that day. Nonetheless, the governor was a great host and showed me his rather large library. We had a good deal of conversation about books and authors. I had now been noticed by two provincial governors—not bad for a poor boy like me.

On the way to Philadelphia, I collected the money owed Vernon at one of our stops. Given Collins's expenses in New York, we couldn't have finished the journey without using some of this money. Collins hoped to find employment as an accounting clerk but no one would hire him, despite some letters of recommendation. Maybe something in his behavior tipped them off to his drinking patterns or maybe he went for his visits with alcohol on his breath. Thus, I continued to pay for his food and lodging. Knowing I had Vernon's money, he continually borrowed some, promising to repay when he gained employment. I gave him so much of it that I became concerned that if asked in the near future to send the money to Vernon, I would be unable to return the entire amount.

Collins kept on drinking and our relationship began to deteriorate as we often fought when he was drunk. The end came as we were boating on the Delaware with some other young men when he said, "I will be rowed home," and refused to take his turn at the oars. I told him in no uncertain terms that we would not row him home. "You will, too, or we'll all spend the night on the water." The others in the boat conceded the matter and agreed to row in his place. But this was the final straw for me and I stood my ground. He became angry and threatened to make me row or throw me overboard. He rushed at me but I dodged, grabbed him by the crotch, and threw him into the river headfirst.

I knew him to be a good swimmer so we rowed the boat a few strokes out of his reach before he could come toward us. Whenever he came near the boat, we asked if he would row before letting him place a hand on the vessel. This made him furious and he stubbornly refused to row. After a long while, he began to tire so we lifted him into the boat and let him make the rest of the trip dripping wet. After this incident, we had few kind words for one another. Collins soon met up with a West India captain who was looking to hire a tutor for the sons of a gentleman in Barbados. Collins agreed to the position and left for the islands. As he departed, he promised to repay me all he owed when he got his first paycheck. Of course, I never heard from him again.

Using Vernon's money as though it were my own—and using it so foolishly—was a big mistake. This incident showed that my father was probably right in supposing me too young to manage my own business. But Sir William read his letter and proclaimed that my father was just too old-fashioned; the governor believed that everyone should be judged on their own merits. He believed that wisdom did not accompany years, nor was youth always without it. "Since he won't set you up," the governor concluded, "I will do it myself!"

Everything to set up a print shop had to be purchased from England in those days. "Give me an inventory of what you need," he said, "and I will get it for you. You can repay me once you become profitable. Philadelphia needs a good printer, and I'm certain that you are the man." He spoke with such sincerity and conviction that I had no doubt that he meant what he said. I was yet to tell anyone about the plans to set me up in Philadelphia. This is one time when staying silent probably did not serve my interests. Had it been known that I was relying on Sir William for help and counsel, maybe a friend who knew the governor's history would have stepped forward to warn me of his tendency to make promises he never meant to keep. Yet, as he came to me first, how could I think this generous offer insincere? I naïvely believed him one of the best men in the world.

I put together an inventory list for the governor that totaled about 100 pounds sterling. Seeing the list, he then surprised me by suggesting that I should travel to England in person to select the equipment rather than order it. He also believed a trip to England would provide me with numerous opportunities to network with booksellers and stationers—potentially valuable customers and suppliers. I could not disagree with his recommendation. "It's settled!" he exclaimed. "Start preparing for the trip because the annual ship between London and Philadelphia sails in a few months." In the meantime, I continued working with Keimer and fretting about the money of Vernon's I had spent on Collins. Every day I feared that it would be called for, but that did not happen for some years after.

> POOR RICHARD ONCE SAID, "HE THAT LIES DOWN WITH DOGS, SHALL RISE UP WITH FLEAS."

CHAPTER 17

The Art of Upward Influence

A feature of Franklin's interpersonal skills is that he was not only effective in persuading peers but also in persuading his superiors. He probably learned these skills in dealings with his father and gained confidence as their relationship matured. In this chapter, he reminds us that influence should flow in both directions on the organizational chart.

KEIMER KNEW NOTHING OF MY PLANS TO set up my own shop, and we got along quite well as a result. He loved to argue so we debated a variety of matters with one another. I worked him over so well with my Socratic method that he began to catch on to the pattern. I often trapped him by asking an apparently random question and then, with related questioning, leading him bit by bit to the point where he began to contradict himself. Eventually, he became cautious and would not answer the most common question without first inquiring as to my intentions for asking it. In the end, our debates gave him such a high opinion of my speaking abilities that he asked me to join him in founding a new religious sect. His role would be to preach all the doctrines, and mine would be to thwart anyone

> **POOR RICHARD ONCE SAID, "EAT TO LIVE, AND NOT LIVE TO EAT."**

who questioned them. The little interest I had in the venture faded as he began to explain his doctrines. Unless we could negotiate a common set of doctrines, I didn't care to go forward.

Two of Keimer's doctrines came from the Mosaic Law. He wore a full-length beard to honor the command, "Thou shalt not mar the corners of thy beard." Likewise, he observed the Sabbath on the seventh day of each week. I disliked both of these but agreed to admit them as common doctrines if he agreed to the doctrine of not eating any sort of meat. He expressed much doubt as to whether his nature could tolerate such a diet. I assured him that it could, and that he would be healthier as a result.

As he was a great glutton, I thought it might be an amusing experiment to put him on a strict vegetarian diet. He agreed to try if I would join him. Always happy for any chance to cut my budget, I quickly agreed and we stayed on it for three months. We contracted with a woman in the neighborhood to prepare and deliver our meals. I gave her 40 vegetarian recipes she could prepare for us.

Since that time, I have often observed this same diet during Lent, making an abrupt transition from my regular diet to a vegetable diet and back again without any side effect whatsoever. My experience in these Lenten observances suggests to me that there's little wisdom in others' advice to ease into transitions. I enjoyed the experiment with Keimer, but he was miserable and longed for any kind of meat. Finally, he could stand it no longer and ordered a roast pig. He invited me and two women friends to join him for the feast. The pig came before we arrived, however, and he could not resist the temptation. He ate the whole pig himself.

Like Keimer, some businesses still choose to observe a Sabbath and close one day each week. Chick-fil-A has closed on Sundays since its founding and enjoys some of the lowest turnover in its industry as a result. Hobby Lobby craft stores closes on Sunday and now operates in 27 states. Of course, banks remain closed on Sundays, too.

CHAPTER 18

---※◆※---

My Friends and Pastimes

*few teenagers these days want to be poets when they grow up. Yet Franklin,
his friends, and his family members all penned a good deal of verse. The
only poetry most businesspeople read today comes on greeting cards. By
contrast, poetry in Franklin's day helped people master the English language and also served as a means of making a personal statement about
how the world worked and which ideals should be pursued. Thus, poetry
readings in those days bore a strange resemblance to what we now refer to
as "developing a personal mission statement." In this chapter, we also meet
Franklin's friends and see how his peers would serve as a source of personal development and, later, strategic information.*

M Y FRIENDS DURING THIS TIME—Charles Osborne, Joseph Watson, and
James Ralph—were all lovers of reading. All three were clerks.
Osborne and Watson worked for Charles Brogdon, a very successful
manuscript copier in Philadelphia, and Ralph worked for a merchant. Watson was a
pious, sensible young man of great integrity. The other two were more lax in their
religious observances, especially Ralph. Osborne was sincere and affectionate as a

friend but could be too frank in matters of literary criticism. Ralph was intelligent, genteel in his manners, and the most eloquent talker I knew at the time. He would, however, cause me as much suffering as John Collins did, and much of it came because neither repaid his debts to me. Both Osborne and Ralph loved poetry and wrote some on occasion. The four of us had many pleasant walks in the woods near the Schuylkill River on Sundays, where we read to one another and then talked about the readings.

Ralph hoped to become a famous poet someday and thereby make his fortune. After all, even great poets have some beginning, said he, and he had already made many of the key mistakes necessary for improvement. Osborne, in contrast, assured him that he had no genius whatsoever for poetry and advised him to stick with the merchant business. A merchant could succeed, he said, through hard work and a good reputation, whereas a poet was subject to a fickle literary public. I couldn't agree more. Although it is fine to amuse oneself with the writing of poetry now and then to improve one's mastery of the English language, one must guard against grander ambitions.

We agreed that each of us should, for our next gathering, compose a bit of verse so that we could read it to one another and improve upon it by our comments. Our goals were only to improve our language and expression, so we ruled out any original compositions. Rather, we agreed that we should all compose a new version of Psalm 18 from the *Holy Bible*, a poem describing the descent of a deity.

Several days before our next meeting, Ralph came to me and informed me that his poem was finished. I replied that I had been too busy with my work to worry about poetry that week. He then asked for my opinion of his poem. I read it and found it to be quite good, in keeping with his eloquent nature. "Help me then," he said. "Out of sheer habit and envy, Osborne will make a thousand criticisms of my work. He is not so jealous of you, however. Would you be willing to take this poem and read it as your own at our next meeting? I will pretend that I didn't have the time to write a poem for this meeting. It will be fun to see how he reacts to the piece this way." We agreed to this plan and I went about transcribing the poem in my own handwriting so as to complete the illusion.

Our meeting arrived and Watson read his poem first. It contained some beautiful lines but mainly defects. Osborne read next and had a much better composition. Ralph made some fair criticisms and also applauded what was worthy in the piece. As planned, he passed on his turn, claiming to have nothing. I read last and feigned disinterest, claiming not to have had sufficient time to perfect the work. My friends allowed me no excuse, however, and forced me to read. The plan was working perfectly.

I read it once and was asked to repeat the performance. Watson and Osborne both proclaimed mine the best of the three and praised the piece extensively. Ralph made some criticisms and recommended improvements—all for show, of course—and I kept the game going by defending the text. Osborne jumped all over Ralph and told him that he was no better a critic than a poet. The two of them walked home together afterwards. Along the way, Osborne continued to rave about my supposed poem, claiming that he restrained his praise earlier so as to not have me think it mere flattery. "Who would have imagined Franklin capable of such poetry?" he declared. "Such beauty . . . such force . . . such fire! He has improved nothing less than the Holy Bible. In his everyday conversation he seems so ordinary. He hesitates; he blunders; and yet—good God!—how he writes!" At our next gathering, Ralph told Osborne about the trick we had played on him, to the accompaniment of no little bit of laughter among us.

> POOR RICHARD ONCE SAID, "GREAT TALKERS, LITTLE DOERS."

This experiment made Ralph more determined than ever to become a poet. I did all I could to discourage him, but he continued composing and publishing verse until a famous poet, Alexander Pope, panned his work in a very public way. Ultimately, he became a good prose writer, and I'll have more to say about him later. The story of my other two friends ends here. Watson, the most upstanding of our group, died in my arms a few years later. Osborne went to the West Indies, where he became a wealthy lawyer, but he also died young. He and I had made a solemn agreement that whoever died first should, if possible, return after death to visit the other and give some account of the afterlife. He has not, as of yet, fulfilled this promise.

CHAPTER 19

Departing for London

In this chapter, the relationship between Franklin and Governor Keith comes to an ugly end and Franklin gets the worst of it. As on his trip from Boston to Philadelphia, Franklin is both wise and humble enough to seek help, and Mr. Denham provides him solid counsel. Despite some setbacks, Franklin is now in the cultural center of the English-speaking world, and he will learn to take full advantage of London's amenities. His time in London reminds us of the transforming power of traveling abroad—regardless of our age.

I BEGAN COURTING MISS DEBORAH READ during these years in Philadelphia. We enjoyed a respect and affection for one another, but I was about to take a long voyage to England. Furthermore, we were both quite young—a bit over 18. Her mother thought it wise to prevent our going too far in the courtship at present. She supposed a marriage would be much more convenient after I returned and set up my own business. Although I was confident of my future, perhaps she, like my father, did not share in my youthful optimism.

Governor Keith liked my company, however, inviting me to his home frequently and always speaking about setting me up in my own business in terms of absolute certainty. For my trip to England, he would furnish me not only with letters of credit to purchase supplies for my print shop but also letters of introduction for a number of his most important friends. These letters always seemed to be forthcoming, and this pattern continued until the day for my departure came. When the ship was set to sail, I desperately called upon his secretary, Dr. Bard, and asked for the letters. Dr. Bard informed me that the governor was busy writing and would catch the ship as it passed by New Castle on the way out of Philadelphia and deliver the letters to me there.

My friend James Ralph, though married and with one child, seemed strangely determined to make this voyage to England with me. I presumed he was going for the purposes of establishing relationships with various merchants in London so as to sell their goods on commission back in America. I would later find out that he was unhappy with both his wife and in-laws, and hoped to leave her on their hands, never to return.

I said farewell to my friends, interchanged some promises with Deborah Read, and left Philadelphia on a ship that soon anchored in New Castle. I went directly to the governor's residence. His secretary very kindly informed me that the governor was present but could not see me as he was engaged in some very important business. He would, however, send the letters to me on board the ship. He wished me a hearty voyage, a speedy return, and many other courtesies. I returned to the ship a bit confused but still not doubting the governor's promise.

The ship was so full of interesting and renowned passengers that Ralph and I had no choice but to room in the steerage. The main cabin was occupied by a group of men, including Mr. Andrew Hamilton, a famous Philadelphia lawyer, and his son James, a future governor; a Quaker merchant, Mr. Denham; and Mr. Onion and Mr. Russel, owners of a large ironworks in Maryland. Colonel French boarded the ship also, and I was accorded a great deal more respect by the other passengers after he greeted me. Mr. Hamilton was called back to Philadelphia before we sailed as he was hired to argue a case concerning a ship seized at sea. This created some room in the main cabin, and Ralph and I were invited by the other occupants to move out of steerage and join them.

Once Colonel French arrived, I approached the captain of the ship and asked for the governor's letters, which were surely under the care of Colonel French.

My intent was to take possession of the letters for the remainder of the voyage. The captain informed me that all of the letters had been put into one bag, to which he did not have easy access at that moment. However, he promised me that before we landed in England I would have the chance to retrieve the letters. Satisfied with his word, we proceeded on our voyage.

The company in the main cabin was excellent and we lived like kings. Having been offered a large fee for his services, Mr. Hamilton left behind a great deal of excellent food and drink he had brought for the voyage. Along the way, Mr. Denham and I began a friendship that would last until his death. In contrast to the company in the main cabin, the voyage was very unpleasant as we were afflicted by much bad weather.

> POOR RICHARD ONCE SAID, "PROMISES MAY GET THEE FRIENDS, BUT NONPERFORMANCE WILL TURN THEM INTO ENEMIES."

As we sailed into the English Channel, the captain kept his word and gave me an opportunity to search the bag for the governor's letters. I could tell by the handwriting that the bag contained several letters written by the governor but none were marked with my name specifically for my oversight. Not to be discouraged, I picked out six or seven letters with the governor's handwriting that seemed to pertain to my situation. For example, one letter was addressed to Mr. Basket, the king's printer. Another was addressed to a local bookseller. We arrived in London on December 24, 1724.

I visited the bookseller first, delivering the letter addressed by Governor Keith. "I don't know any such person," he informed me. Nonetheless, he opened the letter and exclaimed, "Oh, I see. This letter is from that attorney, Mr. Riddlesden. He's a crook and I'll have nothing to do with him or receive letters from him!" With that, he gave me the letter, turned on his heel, and left me to serve a customer. These were clearly not the governor's letters and, after some reflection, I began to doubt his sincerity.

I sought counsel from my new friend, Mr. Denham, and he informed me all about Sir William's character. I learned that nobody relies on the governor's promises and that it was very doubtful that he had written any letters for me. He positively laughed at the idea of the governor giving me a letter of credit as he had no credit whatsoever to give. Gravely concerned with my situation, I asked Denham what I should do. He advised me to find work in the print shops of London. "The print shops are plentiful here and of higher quality than in

America," he said. "If you work a while here before setting up your own shop, you will do so with some degree of competitive advantage."

All of us—Denham, the stationer, and me—knew that Riddlesden was indeed a scoundrel. A few years prior he had conned Mr. Read out of a great deal of money. This accidentally opened letter provided evidence that there was a scheme afoot by the governor and Riddlesden to blacken the reputation of Mr. Hamilton (who was supposed to be traveling with us). Denham, a friend of Hamilton's, thought we ought to bring him up to speed on the matter. So when Mr. Hamilton arrived in England not too much later, I visited him and gave him the letter (which had rightfully been returned to me). He warmly thanked me for such useful information, and returned the favor many times as our friendship developed over the years.

And what are we to think about Governor Keith playing such high-stakes tricks on a naïve boy like me? Let's just say it was a bad habit he had acquired over the years. He wished to please everybody—even teenagers—and having little else to give, gave promises. He was an intelligent, otherwise sensible man, a decent writer, and a good governor for the people, though not for the proprietaries of the Pennsylvania colony, the Penn family, whose instructions he sometimes disregarded. Believe it or not, he authored several of our best laws and passed them during his administration.

—⟫◦⟪—

CHAPTER 20

Making the Best of It in London

An ocean away from home, with only the friends with whom he sailed, Franklin's prospects might be considered bleak. Nonetheless, he quickly finds work, begins writing again, and starts networking throughout London—not bad for a 19-year-old. Living in London was surely a business education for Franklin, for as Daniel Defoe noted, the London of 1724 was driven by "trade, commerce, and the stock market." Incidentally, the asbestos purse he mentions at the end of this chapter is now in the collection at the Natural History Museum of London. You can see a photo of it online in the museum's Picture Library: http://www.nhm.ac.uk/.

JAMES RALPH AND I BECAME INSEPARABLE companions when we set up in London. We acquired modestly priced accommodations together in Little Britain. He requested help from some nearby relatives, but they were poor and unable to offer any assistance. It was at this point that he revealed to me his true intentions of staying in London and never returning to Philadelphia. He had no money with him because he had spent all he had paying for his passage across the

the Atlantic. I had a decent sum of money, so he borrowed from me occasionally as he looked for work. He went first to the theater to look for work, believing himself qualified to be an actor. One of the owners with whom he interviewed advised him rather frankly to drop the idea as he would never succeed in the business. He then proposed a new venture to one of the local publishers to write a new weekly paper somewhat like the very popular *Spectator*. The publisher, however, did not like the idea. After this, Ralph tried to find employment as a temporary writer making copies for some of the booksellers and lawyers. Like the others, this search yielded no results.

In contrast, I found work immediately at the print shop of a Mr. Palmer. It was one of the best shops in all of London, and I worked there for almost a year. I worked hard but spent a good deal of my wages going to plays and other amusements with Ralph. Between the two of us, we consumed all the money I carried over with me and were now living payday to payday. He seemed to forget quickly about his wife and child and I, little by little, grew less attached to Deborah Read. During my time in London, I wrote her only one letter and that to say that I didn't expect to return anytime soon. This would prove to be a great mistake in my life and one I would correct if I had the chance to live that part of my life over again. Worse still, I never had enough money for a return trip to America given the many frivolous expenses we incurred.

> POOR RICHARD ONCE SAID, "BEWARE OF LITTLE EXPENSES, A SMALL LEAK WILL SINK A GREAT SHIP."

Palmer put me to work setting type for the second edition of Wollaston's book, *Religion of Nature*. By the end of the job I'd become quite familiar with Wollaston's book. I found some of his arguments a bit hard to defend, so I composed a short metaphysical pamphlet in which I critiqued his ideas. I dedicated it to James Ralph, titled it "A Dissertation on Liberty and Necessity, Pleasure and Pain," and printed a small number. Mr. Palmer saw it and now perceived me as quite an intelligent young man. He took offense, however, at a number of the arguments and principles contained in my pamphlet and debated them with me. I later considered my printing of this pamphlet a mistake, and I burned as many copies as I could retrieve.

My neighbor in Little Britain was a bookseller named Wilcox. We became acquainted with one another and I discovered that he had a large collection of used books. We agreed to some very reasonable terms which allowed me to take, read, and return any of the books I pleased. This arrangement—which preceded the invention of the circulating library—proved very useful to me.

My pamphlet fell into the hands of a Mr. Lyons, a surgeon and author of a book entitled *The Infallibility of Human Judgment*. He liked what he read and invited me to visit with him to converse on other subjects. He took me to the Horns, a very fashionable alehouse, and introduced me to his friend Dr. Mandeville, author of the *Fable of the Bees*. Mandeville had a private salon there and proved to be a facetious and entertaining companion. Lyons also introduced me to Dr. Pemberton, who in turn promised to introduce me sometime to Sir Isaac Newton. This latter possibility greatly excited me but never came to pass.

I had brought over with me from America a few curiosities, the most unique of which was a purse made of asbestos which could not be burned by fire. Sir Hans Sloane heard about it, came to visit me, and ultimately invited me to his house in Bloomsbury Square. He had quite a collection of curiosities and he persuaded me to add my asbestos purse to his collection. He paid me handsomely for the privilege.

———◦∞◦———

CHAPTER 21

Another Friendship Ends

Franklin once again presents a rather unflattering portrait of himself in this chapter, demonstrating to every reader the folly of mixing money and friendship. Franklin's move to John Watts's print shop probably did more to develop his skills as a printer than anything else he did in London.

THERE WAS A YOUNG WOMAN LODGING in the same house from which we rented our rooms. She was a milliner and, as I recall, had a shop nearby where she sold her wares. She came from a good family, seemed sensible, and was a fun and lively conversationalist. Ralph began reading plays to her in the evening and they soon grew intimate. She began renting at another house, he followed her, and they lived together for some time. However, he was still not working and her income was not enough to sustain the two of them along with the child she brought to the relationship. Thus, Ralph left London to seek a job at a country school.

He thought himself well qualified to be a schoolmaster as he had excellent penmanship and knew quite a bit of math from his work experience in accounting houses. More and more he looked down upon working as a mere businessman and grew increasingly confident that his fortunes lay elsewhere. To be sure his past did not follow him, he changed his name and did me the dubious honor of assuming mine. Not long after his leaving, he sent me a letter informing me that he was settled in the village of Berkshire. He taught reading and writing to about a dozen boys for a modest weekly fee. He asked me to look after his new female friend and to write him with the news, addressing my letters to "Mr. Franklin, Schoolmaster."

Letter after letter followed, each containing a new portion of an epic poem he was composing. He wanted my remarks and corrections, which I gave him from time to time. However, I generally endeavored to dissuade him from becoming a poet. Edward Young had just published a new satire poking fun at anyone who dreamed of making his fortune as a poet. I sent a copy of it to Ralph but he did not yet take Young's hint that, "Fame and fortune are both made of prose." Reams of poetry continued to pour in with every visit from the postman. In the meantime, his female friend had lost both her friends and her business on account of their relationship. She was often in distress and came to me frequently wanting to borrow money. I began to take a liking to her and mistook her desperation for money as admiration for me. Being under no religious restraint at that time in my life, I suggested that we sleep with each other—which ended up being another big mistake.

She rejected me with a proper resentment and informed Ralph of what I had done. On his next trip to London, he informed me that my behavior had cancelled any obligation he had to me. By this he meant that I should never expect to receive any of the money I had lent him. This was, at best, a symbolic punishment because he was clearly unable to repay the monies anyway. Along with the dissolution of the friendship, I found myself relieved of a burden on my pocketbook. I now set my mind to saving some money. Also desiring better work, I left Palmer's print shop to work at the shop of Mr. Watts, the most prestigious in London. I continued at Watts's shop the rest of my stay in London.

> POOR RICHARD ONCE SAID, "A FALSE FRIEND AND A SHADOW, ATTEND ONLY WHILE THE SUN SHINES."

CHAPTER 22

Beer and Productivity

Beer was a fact of life in London print shops long before Franklin arrived on the scene. Once again in his autobiography, Franklin underscores for his readers the dangers of drunkenness and addiction. Franklin saw fondness for too much drink as both an expensive habit and a cruel master. In this chapter, he also shows us both the right way and the wrong way to persuade one's fellow workers. His solution to a rather thorny problem rests on the power of freedom and the power of reason— two cornerstones of the American Experiment.

IN THE PRINT SHOPS OF LONDON, ONE MUST choose between the sedentary work of setting type or the more vigorous job of working the press. In America, one gets to do both jobs. Here, I chose to work the press so I could enjoy the bodily exercise. There was another key difference between this shop and the ones I knew in America. This shop housed nearly 50 workers, and they drank beer all day long as they worked. In contrast, I drank only water. Noting this difference, my fellow workers began to call me the "Water American."

Every now and then, I carried two large sets of type up and down the stairs—one in each hand. My English colleagues, in contrast, carried but one using both hands. They marveled at my strength from this and other demonstrations and wondered aloud how I could be stronger than they. After all, they drank strong beer and I drank only water! A nearby alehouse employed a boy seemingly full-time whose only job was to keep the 50 workers in this shop supplied with beer. This was no small task as each day my companion at the press drank a pint before breakfast, a pint with his breakfast of bread and cheese, a pint between breakfast and lunch, a pint at lunch, a pint in the afternoon about six o'clock, and another pint when he had finished his day's work.

I thought the custom detestable, but my colleague held onto the idea that strong beer made him strong for his labor. I countered that the energy given the body by anything consumed could only be in proportion to the amount of grain or barley flour contained therein. As such, there was more flour—and ener-gy—in a loaf of bread than in a quart of beer, as beer consisted mainly of flour dissolved in water. And, penny for penny, bread was by far the more economical alternative. He drank on, however, and a good portion of his pay each Saturday went to pay his bill for that muddling liquor. I had no such expense and thus avoided the disgrace suffered by many of the workers of being continually in debt.

After some time, Watts, the shop's master, wanted me to leave the pressroom and work setting type in the composing room. This caused a new problem as, unlike in the pressroom, anyone working in the composing room was required to pay five shillings a day for his food and beer. To me, this forced payment bordered on tyranny and, as was my custom, I rebelled. I had set up my own meal plan—far cheaper—while working in the pressroom. I appealed to Watts and he agreed with me, and forbid my paying this fee. For two to three weeks my fellow workers treated me as an excommunicate, and I suffered from a good deal of sabotage. Any time I left the room, I would return to find my type in disarray, my pages transposed, and other such mischief. All of this was ascribed to the "Print Shop Ghost," who haunted all those who refused to be in fellowship with their colleagues. Ultimately, I found Watts's support to be of little consolation and I began to pay their fee. This taught me that it is foolish to be on bad terms with those whom one must live with continually—even when one's principle is sensible.

Paying the fee admitted me to their fellowship, and I soon acquired considerable influence among them. I proposed some reasonable changes to the rules governing this part of the printshop—the mandatory fee and menu being one— and carried them against all opposition. People now had a choice: They could continue having the muddling breakfast of beer, bread, and cheese from the alehouse or—along with me—purchase a breakfast from a different vendor, consisting of a large bowl of hot-water gruel with crumbled bread and a bit of butter and pepper on top.

> POOR RICHARD ONCE SAID, "HE THAT DRINKS FAST, PAYS SLOW."

My breakfast cost less than one pint of beer and kept their heads clearer. Those who continued drinking beer all day habitually ran out of both money and credit from the alehouse. Desperate for drink, they began borrowing money from me, and at interest. I stood at the pay table each Saturday night, collecting from each what they owed me, and used the money to pay their excessive tabs at the alehouse. The beer drinkers were now indebted to me, and the remainder considered me an interesting and witty colleague. My place in their fellowship was now secure. My exceptional speed at typesetting put me in good favor with Mr. Watts, as did my never missing work on Monday from drinking too much on Sunday (like some of my colleagues). From time to time, he would have me do the delivery work, which generally paid better. All things considered, things were going very well for me.

CHAPTER 23

More Tales of My Frugality

Franklin avoided drinking too much alcohol because it was so expensive. In this chapter, he shares with us a few more stories of his frugality. After all, years later he would make famous the phrase, "A penny saved is a penny earned." Here also Franklin shows us that a good relationship is often the best leverage in a negotiation. Some might think that the hard-nosed bargainer gets the best deals, but Franklin is happy to demonstrate otherwise. Social scientists who study persuasion call this the power of liking. That is, if people like you, you have more power in the relationship.

ONCE JAMES RALPH HAD DEPARTED, I BEGAN to think my lodging in Little Britain as too remote. So I found another place much closer to my work. It was on the third floor at the back of an old warehouse. An elderly widow lady owned the building. She had a daughter, a maid, and a worker who attended to the business of the warehouse but lodged elsewhere. She checked my reputation with my current landlord and agreed to take me in at the same modest rate. Both she and I thought it a bargain, as I paid the same but walked less, and she now had a man on the property to help protect the place.

She was the daughter of a Protestant clergyman but had been converted to Catholicism by her dearly departed husband. In her younger days, she had spent a great deal of time among famous people and knew a thousand good stories about them, going back some 50 to 60 years. She seldom left her room as she could hardly walk owing to being diseased with the gout. She delighted in having company, and I found hers so amusing that I would spend an evening with her whenever she desired it.

On these evenings we shared a light supper of half of an anchovy each on a small strip of bread with butter and a half pint of ale. Her conversation was the only entertainment we needed. She enjoyed me as a tenant and was very unwilling to see me go, as I never stayed out late nor gave hardly any trouble. Once when I talked of renting a different room closer to my business and even cheaper than this one, she persuaded me otherwise. She countered at a price even lower than my new alternative, and so I stayed with her for the rest of my stay in London at a price of less than half of what I had started out paying.

Another room in my landlady's house was occupied by a 70-year-old woman who had never married. My landlady told me that this woman was also Catholic and had been sent abroad at a young age, where she lived in a nunnery and hoped to become a nun. She discovered that she did not like her new country and returned to England. Since England had no nunneries, she vowed to live as close to the life of a nun as she could in her home country.

> POOR RICHARD ONCE SAID, "WOULD YOU LIVE WITH EASE, DO WHAT YOU OUGHT, AND NOT WHAT YOU PLEASE."

To fulfill this pledge, she gave away her entire estate to charity, keeping only twelve pounds a year to live on. Even out of this small sum, she gave a great deal to charity. She ate only hot-water gruel and made no fire except to boil this. She had lived many years in a small, upper room and made hardly any noise. In addition, she never paid rent as the series of Catholic owners of the property considered it a blessing to have her live in the house. A priest visited her once a day to hear her confession. My landlady once asked her, given her lifestyle, why she needed daily confessionals with a priest. "Oh," she responded, "I find it impossible to not think myself better than others."

Once I was permitted to visit her. She was a cheerful and polite hostess and we conversed pleasantly. The room was clean and had no furnishings other than a mattress, a table holding a crucifix and a book, a stool, and a picture over the fireplace of Saint Veronica holding up her handkerchief displaying the miraculous figure of Christ's bleeding face. She explained this picture to me in all manner of seriousness. She looked pale, but apparently suffered no illness whatsoever. It reminded me yet again of how little it takes to get by in life.

Hewlett-Packard CEO Mark Hurd had a reputation for frugality long before he took over the company in 2005 after Carly Fiorina's departure. His college friends told reporters that Hurd could buy more food for $1.89 than anyone else they knew.

CHAPTER 24

The End of the London Adventure

Had things happened a bit differently in London, Franklin might never have returned to America, and we would have been without one of our most interesting and valuable citizens. Thankfully, this did not happen, and Franklin gives us a glimpse in this chapter of two of the roads not taken. Once again, he demonstrates the power of being likable and shows how this can open doors. It's also impressive that Franklin managed in his later years to speak well of people who caused him misery in his early years—like John Collins and James Ralph. Maybe he's trying to teach us that a balanced view of human beings helps us keep our balance in difficult situations.

WHILE WORKING AT WATTS'S PRINT SHOP, I made friends with a well-educated young man named Wygate. Coming from a wealthy family, he had been better educated than most printers. He knew Latin, spoke French, and loved reading. Like me, he desired to be master of his own shop one day and we studied many of the same areas. I taught him and a friend how to swim in only two lessons, and they soon became excellent swimmers.

One day we all traveled with some wealthy friends of theirs along the river to Chelsea to see some curiosities on display at the college there. Wygate greatly excited the entire company on our return trip about my swimming abilities. At the request of the group, I stripped down, leaped into the river, and swam from Chelsea all the way to Blackfryar's—a distance of about three and one-half miles. Along the way, I performed many interesting feats both upon and under the water that pleased everyone, as such was a novelty in that day.

I'd loved swimming ever since childhood and had mastered all of the most important motions and positions. I had even invented a few of my own, aiming at the graceful and easy as well as the practical. I exhibited all of these to our company that day and was flattered by their admiration. Shortly after this trip, Wygate proposed that the two of us travel all over Europe together, supporting ourselves as necessary by working in print shops. I liked the idea and mentioned it to my good friend Mr. Denham at our next meeting. He dissuaded me from going, advising me instead to concentrate on returning with him to Philadelphia.

Denham was a man of remarkable character, as this next story demonstrates. Earlier in his life, he failed in business while living in Bristol, and his creditors could do little but write off the loans when he left for America to begin things anew. Once across the Atlantic, he avoided making the same mistakes in his new business as a merchant. As such, he acquired a large fortune in a rather short period of time. His first return to London was on the ship that carried me there. After arriving, he invited his former creditors to a dinner at which he thanked them for their previous support. Expecting nothing beyond his gratitude and the dinner, each man there found under his plate a money order for the full amount of the original debt, plus interest.

He now informed me that he was about to return to Philadelphia with a great quantity of goods and open a store there. He invited me to join him as his clerk—keeping his books, copying his letters, and attending to the store in his absence. As soon as I learned his business, he would help set me up with my own store in the West Indies. If I managed myself well there, he believed, I would establish my fortune. I liked the sound of his proposal as I had grown tired of London. I remembered with pleasure the happy months I had spent in Philadelphia, and I longed to see the place again. Thus, I agreed to his proposal on the spot for 50 Pennsylvania pounds a year. This was less than my current wages but offered much better prospects for me.

I resigned my post at Watts's shop and took leave of printing forever, or so I thought at the time. I now went about with Mr. Denham each day purchasing articles from the tradesmen. My new work varied from monitoring the packing of the goods, to doing errands, to managing deliveries to the ship. Everything went smoothly and I found myself with a few days of leisure before the ship sailed.

> POOR RICHARD ONCE SAID, "ALL THINGS ARE EASY TO INDUSTRY, ALL THINGS ARE DIFFICULT TO SLOTH."

Much to my surprise, I was called to visit a rather important man on one of these days. Sir William Wyndham had somehow heard of my swimming exploits on the trip from Chelsea and of my teaching Wygate and his friend to swim in only two lessons. He had two sons about to set out on their own travels. If I taught them how to swim, he would pay me very handsomely. They were not yet in town, and because I knew I only had a few days before the ship sailed I turned down his very generous offer. This incident made me wonder whether I should stay in England and open a swimming school. I thought the prospects so strong at the time that I would probably have stayed if his offer had been made to me sooner. Had I succeeded at this undertaking, I may never have returned to America.

Thus I spent about 18 months in London, working hard at my business much of the time. What little I spent on myself went for plays and books. My friend James Ralph had kept me poor and owed me an amount equal to half of my current annual wages. This was a lot of money, and I was never going to see any of it again. I loved him nonetheless for he had many likable qualities. I had by no means improved my fortune on this adventure, but I had read a great deal. As important, I had improved the quality of my social network immeasurably, and benefited greatly from the counsel of these new friends.

PART II

The Rise of an Entrepreneur

CHAPTER 25

Setting a Course and Staying Flexible

The 20-year-old Franklin could return to Philadelphia proud of what he had accomplished in London. Denham was a model of Quaker virtues like hard work and honesty, and his inclusion in the autobiography proves his lasting influence on Franklin's life. Denham's unexpected death would be another blow, but the ever resourceful Franklin moves on.

In the first paragraph, Franklin mentions a plan he created to guide his conduct in life. Surprisingly, he never included this in his autobiography. Here is that four-part plan. Notice how Franklin viewed this voyage back to America as a new beginning for himself.

"Those who write about poetry teach us that the greatest poems always began with a grand design or plan. Without these, a poem would just be a hodgepodge of scenes. It is the same with life. I have never had a plan for my life. As a result, it has been as confusing as a poem littered with unconnected events. This voyage back home is a chance to start anew. Therefore, I'm going to make some resolutions and set forth a plan to govern my new life so that I might live rationally and intentionally.

1. It is necessary for me to be extremely frugal for some time, until I have paid all my debts.

2. *I'll do my best to speak the truth in every situation. I'll also seek to avoid giving people expectations that are unlikely to be met, aiming instead at complete sincerity in every word and action. Such is the most excellent pursuit for a rational being.*

3. *I plan to work very hard at whatever business I undertake in the future. I will not distract myself from my business by any foolish scheme for getting rich quickly. Hard work and patience are the most certain ways to wealth.*

4. *Finally, I resolve never to speak poorly of anyone, not even in a matter of the truth. Instead, I will choose by some means to excuse the faults I hear charged upon others, and whenever possible speak all the good I know of everybody."*

WE SAILED FROM ENGLAND ON JULY 23, 1726. I recorded all the activities of that voyage in my personal journal, and you may find the stories there. Perhaps the most important thing I did on that particular voyage across the Atlantic was to create a plan to guide my future conduct in life. In retrospect, I find the plan remarkable for two reasons. First, I developed it at the young age of 20. Second, I adhered to it rather faithfully across the course of my life.

We landed in Philadelphia on October 11th. Much had changed in my 18 months abroad. Sir William Keith was no longer governor, having been replaced by Major Gordon. Governor Keith and I met on the streets as common citizens one day. He seemed ashamed to see me and passed without a word. Given all the promises I made to her, I would have been just as ashamed to see Deborah Read had she not been persuaded to marry in my absence. She married a man named Rogers, a potter, not long after receiving my one and only letter written to her from London. Her marriage to him was both brief and unhappy. She moved out and refused to keep his name when word began to spread that he now had two wives. His fine reputation as a workman had persuaded her to marry him, but his moral ethic clearly did not equal his work ethic. Soon after she left him, he got too deep into debt, ran away to the West Indies, and died there.

My former master, Keimer, had moved his shop to better quarters, supplied it well with paper and plenty of new types, and now had a number of new hands (though none were very good). Business for him had never been better. Mr. Denham opened his new store on Water Street, and I started learning my new business.

I watched the store, did the accounting, and soon became an expert salesman. Denham and I lived together during this time and he was like a father to me. I loved him as a son and we might have gone on together into the future had tragedy not struck. Just after I turned 21 years old, we both became severely ill—mine was pleurisy. I suffered much and I came so close to dying that I actually resigned myself to the possibility. My unexpected recovery brought with it a bit of disappointment—namely, that I would have to go through the wretched process of dying again some day. I've now forgotten what illness carried Denham off, but he suffered with it a long time before he succumbed. His final act of kindness was leaving me a small legacy in his oral will. The executors of his will took over his store, however, and I was once again turned out to the wide world when my employment there ended.

> POOR RICHARD ONCE SAID, "LOOK BEFORE, OR YOU'LL FIND YOURSELF BEHIND."

My brother-in-law, Captain Holmes, now lived in Philadelphia and advised me to return to my original business of printing. Keimer also tempted me with a handsome annual wage to come manage his print shop so he could attend to his new stationer's shop. Keimer's wife and her friends still lived in London and I had heard many bad things about him and his business during my time there. Not wanting to have anything more to do with him, I tried to continue my work started under Denham and find employment as a merchant's clerk. Having no success, I resigned myself to returning to Keimer's shop.

He employed the following people at the time:

- Hugh Meredith, a 30-year-old Welsh Pennsylvanian bred to country work; honest, sensible, somewhat of a reader with an instinct for business, but given to drink.
- Stephen Potts, a country boy in his early 20's; born to be a farmer, he enjoyed a solid build with great wit and a good sense of humor; hardly ever idle.
- John, a wild Irishman trained in no business whatsoever; Keimer had purchased four years of his service from the captain of a ship and he worked the press with Meredith.
- George Webb, an Oxford scholar; Keimer had also purchased four years of his service from a sea captain wishing to have him work in composition, setting types.
- David Harry, a country boy who Keimer had taken as an apprentice.

Meredith and Potts had agreed to work for Keimer starting at extremely low weekly wages. Their pay would be raised one shilling every three months if they improved their skills and deserved the raise. Apparently, the expectation of higher wages in this contract drew them in. Meredith was to work at the press and Potts at bookbinding. Keimer had promised to teach them both, and he unfortunately knew neither skill himself. I soon realized that his purpose in hiring me at such high wages was to have me train his cheap new labor, turn me out, and place his workers under indentured contracts. Nevertheless, I went about my work cheerfully making order out of his chaotic shop, and these workers improved their skills under my tutelage.

It was certainly an odd thing to find an Oxford scholar like George Webb in the situation of a bought service, but then again, he was not yet 18. He told me he was born in and educated at a prep school in Gloucester. His teachers thought him to be superior as he had published a few pieces of prose and verse in the local newspapers, and he was an exceptionally talented actor in the local theater. He was sent to Oxford and hated his first year in school, wishing nothing other than to go to London and become an actor. Receiving his quarterly allowance one day, he used it to do just that, rather than paying off his debts.

Having no mentor in London, he soon fell into bad company, spent all his money, and never gained an introduction to the acting troops. His situation grew so desperate he pawned his good clothing and dressed in rags. Someone put a flyer in his hand as he walked the streets, lost and hungry. It offered immediate food, lodging, and entertainment to anyone who would bind themselves into service on ships bound for America. Desperate for aid, he signed the indentures immediately and was put onto a ship. He left no word and his friends never knew what became of him. I found him to be witty, good-natured company in the shop, but he was an idle worker and clearly irresponsible.

John, the Irishman, broke his indentures and ran away. I got along very well with the other four, and they respected me primarily because Keimer was incapable of instructing them. Under my oversight, they learned something new every day. We worked on neither Sunday, the Christian Sabbath, nor Saturday, as Keimer still kept that day as his Sabbath. This gave me two full days for reading each week and also allowed me to continue seeking the company of intelligent, educated people all over town. For his part, Keimer treated me well both privately and in front of others. The only thing that now bothered me was the money of Vernon's I had spent foolishly on my friends. I still did not have the funds to pay the debt if called upon, but it remained undemanded by its kind and rightful owner.

Our print shop was sorely in need of several letters in our types and no one yet produced typefaces in America. I had watched types being cast while in London but could not recall the exact process. Nevertheless, I invented my own mold, used our current types to punch the letters, and poured new types made of lead. In this manner, I covered our shortages in a tolerable manner. I also engraved pictures on occasion, made ink, and ran the warehouse of supplies. I had become a regular jack-of-all-trades.

> Many great entrepreneurs faced the possibility of an early death. Barbie inventor Ruth Handler survived breast cancer. As a child, Casa Olé founder and Horatio Alger Award winner Tom Harken suffered from both polio and tuberculosis.

CHAPTER 26

The Junto—A Club for Mutual Self-Improvement

At this point in his life, Franklin was an outsider in the business community. He thus lacked the access to information that circulated in the private clubs and meetings of the long-time merchants and businessmen of Philadelphia. Rather than waiting for an invitation from the insiders, he organized his own club for the dual purposes of continued self-development and for gathering strategic knowledge. It's commonly believed that they pronounced the name of their club "June-tow."

IN THE AUTUMN OF 1727, I ORGANIZED MOST OF my educated friends into a club of mutual improvement which we called the Junto. We gathered together every Friday evening, and our meetings were governed by a set of formal rules so that our time would not digress into mere gossip or pointless disputation. Every member would take turns producing one or more position papers on any point of morals, politics, or science to be discussed at our next meeting. Once every quarter, a member could compose and read an original essay on a topic of his choice.

The rules stated that one member would serve as chief facilitator during our debates, and that these were to be conducted in the sincere spirit of inquiry. We were to seek truth, avoiding both the temptation toward dispute or victory. We later amended the rules further to dissuade anyone from ruining the dialogue and escalating the debate. Anybody expressing their opinions as firm, or habitually contradicting another's statement was forced to pay a small fine.

> POOR RICHARD ONCE SAID, "HE THAT WON'T BE COUNSELL'D, CAN'T BE HELP'D."

The founding members were:

- Hugh Meredith, Stephen Potts, and George Webb, whom I have previously described in detail.
- Joseph Breintnall, a copier of deeds for the public copiers and a friendly middle-aged man. Joseph read all the poetry he could find and even wrote some decent verse himself. He was a veritable fountain of trivia and tended toward wisdom in his conversation.
- Thomas Godfrey, a self-taught and very talented mathematician. He would later invent what is now called Hadley's Quadrant, a useful device for navigating the sea. He knew little beyond mathematics and was often irritating in conversation. As with most mathematicians I know, he expected too much precision in all statements and he constantly dwelled on such trifles. We were not too sad to see him leave the group.
- Nicholas Scull, a surveyor who became Surveyor General. He loved reading and sometimes composed a few verses of poetry.
- William Parson, bred a shoemaker but a great lover of reading. His curiosity gave him a good grounding in mathematics. He used this to dabble a bit in astrology, but ultimately laughed at the concept. Like Scull, he became a Surveyor General.
- William Maugridge, a cabinet maker, a talented mechanic, and a man of great integrity.
- Robert Grace, a wealthy young fellow, generous, enthusiastic, and witty. Puns were his talent and he proved to be a loyal friend.
- William Coleman, a merchant's clerk as I had been under Denham. He was about my age and possessed the calmest temperament, the best heart, and the clearest morals of almost any man I had ever met. He went on to become a wealthy merchant and one of our provincial judges. We stayed friends until his death 40 years later.

Our club for mutual improvement lasted for several decades and was the best school of philosophy, morality, and politics that then existed in Pennsylvania. At each meeting, we introduced our topics for the following week and we each prepared carefully for the dialogue. Our rules helped us all acquire better habits of conversation, and we seldom became angry with one another. I have no doubt that such civility was central to the longevity of our club.

CHAPTER 27

Breaking with Keimer and Making My Own Plans

Though Keimer benefited immensely from Franklin's service, Franklin knew all along that the relationship would end at a time of Keimer's choosing. He would not have long to wait. Along the way, Franklin demonstrates the virtue of patience and the value of networking to successfully navigate stormy waters that could have wrecked people of lesser character.

HOWEVER GOOD MY SERVICES, IT WAS clear that Keimer ultimately wished to be rid of me. The day came when he paid me my wages and, feeling them to be too heavy, he desired me to take a cut in pay. Each day thereafter he grew less civil and began flaunting his authority. He constantly found fault with my work, and the situation became more and more volatile. I stayed patient as the situation escalated, hoping that he would realize how much he really needed me. Ultimately, he capitalized on the following petty incident to end our relationship.

One day while I was working, a great noise arose down the street, and I poked my head out of an upper-story window to discover the cause of the commotion. Keimer watched me do this from the street below and yelled at me in an angry tone to mind my own business. Not satisfied, he went on to insult me in front of everyone else, and this really angered me. He marched directly to the print shop to continue the quarrel, and strong words were exchanged by both of us. He warned me again that he was growing weary of my wages and urged me to take the hint. I told him that hinting was no longer necessary and that I would leave him that instant. Taking my hat in hand, I departed, asking only Meredith on the way out to bring my things to my lodgings.

Meredith came that evening, and we talked over the incident. He had great regard for me and wished that I would not leave him alone in that place. He talked me out of returning to Boston, reminding me that Keimer was in debt for all he possessed. Furthermore, his creditors were uneasy as they knew he couldn't keep his shop. He often sold without profit for ready money, trusted both people and memory rather than kept accounts, and would surely go under now that I was not there to help. His fall would be a vacancy from which I could profit.

Though I couldn't disagree with Meredith, I still lacked money. He then let me know that his father held me in high regard and had told Meredith that he would readily lend me money to set up my own shop if I would make Meredith my partner. Meredith said that his contract with Keimer would end in the spring and by that time we could have our press and types sent from London. "I am no great printer like you," he said, "but I know a good business opportunity when I see it. If we combine your abilities and my capital, we can split the profits equally."

I agreed to the proposal, and his father—who happened to be in town—approved it soon after. His father thought me to be a positive influence on his son as I had recently persuaded Meredith to stop drinking. He hoped that I might break him of that self-destructive habit entirely now that we were in business with one another. I gave an inventory to Meredith's father and he carried it to a local merchant, who would send our things from England. The secret would be kept until the goods arrived, and I was to find work at Bradford's shop in the meantime. Bradford had no room for me, however, and so I remained idle for a few days. In the meantime, Keimer started closing a deal to print some paper money for New Jersey and needed work and engravings that only I could supply. Fearful that Bradford would employ me and take this job from him, he sent me a very civil message stating that old friends should not part over a few words said in anger. Would I consider coming back?

Meredith urged me to agree as it would give us the chance to keep working with each other and thereby improve his skills. So I returned and things went as smoothly as they ever had. Keimer landed the New Jersey job, and I invented a copper plate press for it—the first that had been seen in this country. I also created several ornaments and security measures for the bills to make them harder to counterfeit. We all went over to Burlington together, and I completed the job to everyone's satisfaction. Keimer received such a large sum for this job that he was able to keep his head above water much longer than he would have otherwise.

> POOR RICHARD ONCE SAID, "KEEP THY SHOP, & THY SHOP WILL KEEP THEE."

At Burlington, I acquainted myself with many important people of the province. Several of them had been appointed by the Assembly to monitor our press to ensure that we printed no more bills than the law directed. They were, therefore, constantly taking turns watching us, and whoever came to monitor usually brought a friend or two along for company. Everyone seemed to value my conversation over that of Keimer's and this was most likely due to all the reading I had done. I found myself invited to their homes, introduced to their friends, and shown much hospitality. Though Keimer was master of the shop, he was much neglected in Burlington. He was such an odd fellow we shouldn't have expected a different outcome. Keimer never knew the daily news, he loved rudely opposing any stated opinion, he dressed shabbily, had poor hygiene, bordered on fanatical when he practiced religion, and was a bit of a scoundrel at heart.

Our job there lasted three months and, by the end, I counted as my friends Judge Allen, Samuel Bustill (the secretary of the province), Isaac Pearson, Joseph Cooper, several of the Smiths, many members of the Assembly, and Isaac Decow, the Surveyor General. Mr. Decow was a wise old fellow who told me that he got his start wheeling clay for brickmakers. Once old enough to leave home, he learned to write and started carrying chains for the surveyors. They, in turn, taught him how to survey and by working hard he had acquired himself a great fortune. He told me, "I predict that you will soon work this Keimer fellow out of business and make your fortune printing in Philadelphia."

At that time, he had no knowledge of my intention to set up shop. All of these new friends were of great use to me along the way and, in return, I was occasionally of use to them. They all continued their regard for me as long as they lived.

CHAPTER 28

Reflecting on My Morals

Franklin believed that a person's principles and values are central to determining his success. He therefore takes time in this chapter to discuss in detail his principles and morals before giving the story of his rise in business. The story of Franklin's life continues in the next chapter, but Franklin's character development is described in this one.

BEFORE I TELL YOU THE STORY OF MY starting and growing my business, I thought it wise to say something about my principles and morals. If you know about these at the beginning of my business story, you'll see how they shaped all that followed.

As you know, I grew up in a religious home and was reared to be dutiful in my religious observances. About the age of 15, after a good deal of reading, I began to have my doubts that God ever revealed himself to humankind in person or Holy Scripture. I came across some books attempting to refute Deism and they had quite the opposite effect on me. In these books, I found the arguments of the Deists to be stronger than the arguments of those attempting the refutation. In short, I became a Deist.

I soon convinced others of the rightness of Deism, particularly Collins and Ralph, but both of them treated me very poorly in the end. My suspicion of Deism was deepened when I learned that Governor Keith was a Deist, and you now know how he treated me. After reflecting upon my own behavior toward Vernon and Deborah Read, I began to doubt that Deism could serve as the foundation for my moral thinking. Even if Deism were true, it had a poor track record among myself and my acquaintances. By the time I published my pamphlet on morality in London, I had placed these lines from Dryden on the first page:

> Whatever is, is right. Mankind is almost blind and
> Sees but part of the chain, the nearest link:
> His eyes cannot carry to the perfect beam,
> That holds the weight above.

If God indeed has infinite wisdom, goodness, and power, I could only conclude that everything in the world must be good as well. Good and evil now became empty distinctions to me. I formerly put no stock in this idea, assuming it to be more of a clever argument than truth. Now, if true, I believed that everything was good and nothing was evil. This just reminded me how changing one's assumptions can affect all that follows.

I became convinced that truth, authenticity, and integrity in all interpersonal dealings were foundational to success and happiness. I wrote out resolutions to this effect that remain to this day in my private journal, and they have guided

> POOR RICHARD ONCE SAID, "SUCCESS HAS RUIN'D MANY A MAN."

my life since. I no longer believed that the Bible should have any claim on my life just because others held it in high esteem. Certain actions weren't bad only because they were forbidden in the Bible or good only because they were commanded in the Bible. Rather, I came to be of the opinion that certain actions are forbidden because they are bad for us, and certain actions are commanded because they are good for us. There appeared to be rational laws governing the moral world, and the more we conformed our lives to these, the better our lives would be.

These convictions coupled with the kind hand of Providence—or some guardian angel, or good fortune, or all of it together—preserved me through my youth. I survived many a difficult situation among strangers, far removed from the protection and advice of my father. The mistakes and errors I have noted in this text were not the willful acts of immorality or the injustice that one might expect from a youth without a religion. I say "willful" because the instances I have mentioned thus far were all driven by circumstantial necessity (youth, inexperience, and others taking advantage of me), not my own willful disobedience. If nothing else, I became aware of the power of a good reputation very early in my life and became determined to preserve mine.

The scandals that plagued the United States' economy in the early years of the 21st century created a crisis of trust in corporate leadership. President George W. Bush addressed this crisis of corporate responsibility, contending that the strength of the American economy depends on "the ethical standards . . . upheld by responsible business leaders." He further argued that "ultimately the ethics of American business depend on the conscience of American business leaders." Like Franklin, every entrepreneur and businessperson must think deeply about their ethical standards.

CHAPTER 29

Getting Started

Franklin writes in this chapter of a kind favor done for him just after he set up his own shop. Recalling it 50 years later, he still appreciates the person who helped him. Such stories challenge us to ask ourselves, "Whom can I help today?" Lending a helping hand to a beginner often costs us little and is long remembered. He goes on to show us the power of a good reputation and also provides a memorable portrait of a pessimist who tried to discourage him. Even though Philadelphia was coming out of a depression at the time, great leaders like Franklin always find a way to frame a positive future.

OUR TYPES AND EQUIPMENT ARRIVED FROM London not long after we returned to Philadelphia from the New Jersey job. Meredith and I settled matters with Keimer and, with his consent, left his shop for good. We rented a house near the market and set up our shop. The rent was rather high—and it has since nearly tripled—so we subleased part of the place to Thomas Godfrey, a glass maker. He boarded his family in the unused portion of the house and paid us a considerable part of the rent. On top of this, Meredith and I boarded with the family.

We had hardly put our equipment in order before a friend of mine brought us our first customer: a gentleman needing five shillings' worth of printing. Coming on the heels of our considerably large capital outlay to open the shop, this gentleman's modest purchase coming so quickly after our opening gave me more pleasure than any big contract I have since landed. The gratitude I felt toward my friend who brought this business to us taught me that favors done for young beginners are long remembered and always repaid.

The Junto provided much more for me than just interesting conversation. Each of us worked hard to bring business to one another. In fact, Breintnall managed to get us a good bit of business from the Quakers who were at the time printing some of their history. They drove a hard bargain and we had to work quickly if the job was to be profitable to us. They desired a rather large book with small type. My goal was to set into type two pages of it each day and then Meredith would run it through the press. During this time, we often worked past eleven at night before the day's work was done because we had other small jobs coming in from our other friends.

At the end of all my efforts one night, I accidentally knocked over two typeset pages of my day's work. The pages were hopelessly scrambled by the mishap, but I was determined to stay on my pace. I set the pages again immediately before going to bed. Our late-night industriousness was visible to everyone in the neighborhood and our reputation—and credit—only improved as a result. In particular, I was told that our new print shop had become a frequent topic of conversation each evening among the local merchants at the social

> POOR RICHARD ONCE SAID, "EARLY TO BED AND EARLY TO RISE, MAKES A MAN HEALTHY, WEALTHY AND WISE."

club. The general opinion was that we were destined to fail as there were already two printers in Philadelphia (Keimer and Bradford). One merchant, Dr. Baird, disagreed with this, however. He told the other merchants, "Franklin's work ethic is better than that of anybody I've seen. Every night when I come to the club, he's still at work. And the next morning, he's at work again before his neighbors are even out of bed." The other merchants must have listened closely because one of them soon approached us in hopes of being our paper and ink supplier. Yet, none of them chose to send any work to our shop.

Although it seems as if I'm only praising myself, I mention this story about my work ethic so that my posterity, who read my story one day, may have a clear idea as to the benefit of that virtue. Industriousness served me well all my life, and you'll hear more of it and its rewards in future chapters.

Every place has its pessimist who's quick to proclaim impending disaster. In Philadelphia this person was Samuel Mickle. Mickle was a well-known, elderly man with a wise look and a very serious manner of speaking. I did not know Mickle at the time, but he stopped by our print shop one afternoon and asked me if I was the young man who had just opened the new print shop. I told him I was, and he said that he was very sorry for me. Knowing printing to be an expensive undertaking, he informed me that my investment would soon be lost because Philadelphia was about to collapse. Half the people in the city were on the verge of bankruptcy, and the current construction boom and rise in rents was, in reality, only an investment scheme that would soon ruin us all.

He continued giving me so many stories of misfortune—present or expected—that I became rather depressed after his visit. Had I sought his counsel prior to my setting up, I certainly never would have taken the risk. Mickle continued to reside in the reputedly decaying city of Philadelphia for many years, refusing to buy a house so as to avoid financial ruin when the bottom fell out. Years later he relented, and I had the pleasure of watching him pay five times as much for a house as what he would have paid had he been more optimistic from the beginning.

CHAPTER 30

A Strategic Response to a Competitive Betrayal

Franklin started publishing his own newspaper, The Pennsylvania Gazette, *in 1729 and his acquisition of the paper is an interesting story indeed. He had the idea first, but it was stolen from him through an error of trust on his part. Rather than suing, Franklin decides to address the matter in the marketplace with a most creative response to a nasty competitive betrayal. In the end, he took control of* The Pennsylvania Gazette *and it became the most widely read newspaper in the colonies during the next decade.*

SOMEWHAT UNEXPECTEDLY, MR. VERNON SENT a gentle notice to me about the money I collected for him earlier that I now owed him. Knowing it had been years since I retrieved it for him, he did not press me. I wrote him a clear and concise letter of acknowledgment in which I asked him for some patience as the time had indeed been long. Thus, I was able, along with many thanks, to repay him the money with interest. Although I couldn't return to my earlier life and make better decisions, that mistake was now somewhat corrected.

About the same time, a female patron lent George Webb the money necessary to purchase his time from Keimer. He offered his services to us as a journeyman, but we did not have enough business to employ him. As a foolish gesture of consolation, I informed him that we intended to start a newspaper soon and this might provide enough work for him. The only newspaper at the time was printed by Bradford. By anyone's standards it was a dull, pathetic, paper and poorly managed—yet somehow still profitable. Competing against him with a quality newspaper would surely make money.

I asked Webb to keep the matter a secret, but he told Keimer who immediately tried to preempt me by publishing proposals announcing his intentions to the public. Webb, of course, would be employed as a journeyman to manage the undertaking. I was furious. We could not yet begin our own paper, so I set about to counteract their efforts by publishing several clever essays in Bradford's paper using the name "Busy Body." My friend Breintnal continued the essays for some months.

It worked like a charm. The public suddenly became enamored with Bradford's paper and Keimer's proposals were disregarded—after, of course, a thorough ridiculing of them in our "Busy Body" column. Nevertheless, Keimer began his paper and kept it going for nine months on—at most—90 subscribers. Frustrated with his progress, he offered to sell the paper to me for an extremely small fee. Having been ready for some months to get my own paper going, I took him up on the offer, and this newspaper proved extremely profitable to me within a few years.

The first papers we printed made quite a splash throughout Pennsylvania. They were set in better type, were more clearly printed, and contained some of my most spirited writing. One of my political essays focused on a current dispute between the governor of Massachusetts, William Burnet, and the Massachusetts Assembly. Everyone who read it found it thought-provoking, especially the people in Massachusetts engaged in the conflict. As a result, our paper—and its managing editor—were the talk of the town. Within a few weeks, everyone involved in the conflict had become a subscriber.

I kept to this strategy and our subscription base continued to grow. Suddenly, all the work I had put into developing a provocative writing style—all those hours spent copying the *Spectator* essays—seemed to pay off. Better still, the leaders in the community were pleased to see good writing in a newspaper and began both to subscribe and encourage me. By contract, Bradford's newspaper had long printed the votes, the laws, and other public business of the House. At one point he printed, poorly and with many errors, a speech given to the governor by the House.

We seized the opportunity to reprint the speech elegantly and correctly and sent one copy to every member of the House. Everyone noticed the difference in quality immediately, and it made us many friends in the House. In fact, they voted us—instead of Bradford—their printers for the next year. Among my friends in the House I must mention again Mr. Hamilton, the lawyer whom I helped on my trip to London a few years earlier. He had long since returned from England and now had a seat in the House. He was of great help to me in gaining the public contracts in this situation and he continued helping me in such matters until his death many years later.

> POOR RICHARD ONCE SAID, "THREE MAY KEEP A SECRET IF TWO ARE DEAD."

Soon the people of Pennsylvania demanded the printing of more paper money for the province. Years before, 15,000 pounds of paper money had been floated and it was slowly disappearing. The wealthy people of the province opposed all forms of paper currency because they believed it caused all money to depreciate in value to the ultimate ruin of both lenders and borrowers.

We discussed this point in our Junto and I came down on the side of printing more paper money. After all, following the initial float of 15,000 pounds six years earlier, the province had increased in trade, employment, and population. When I first walked the streets of Philadelphia with those bread rolls under each arm, I noticed numerous "For Rent" signs on the doors of the houses in the commercial district. Now, not only were these old houses inhabited, but many new ones were being built. This indicated that the province enjoyed a healthy economy.

Our debates excited me so much that I wrote and anonymously printed a pamphlet on the subject entitled "The Nature and Necessity of a Paper Currency." The rich despised it, but it was well received by all others in the community. It definitely fueled the public outcry for more money, and the wealthy of the area had no writers in their midst able to refute the arguments. Their opposition began to slacken and the majority vote in the House settled the matter on the side of printing more money. Still finding me to be of service, my friends in the House

Sometimes the wheels of justice in the marketplace grind faster than the wheels of justice in court. When betrayed by a pair of business colleagues, Cornelius Vanderbilt wrote them saying, "Gentlemen: You have undertaken to cheat me. I won't sue you, for the law is too slow. I'll ruin you." And he went to work immediately to make this happen.

gave me the printing job. It was a lucrative contract and it helped me greatly. Once again, my writing exercises paid a nice return on the time and effort invested.

Over time, the benefits of a paper currency grew increasingly clear to everyone in the province. In fact, it was never a matter of much dispute after this point. It soon grew to 55,000 pounds and then, in 1739, to 80,000 pounds. During the war with the French and Indians it went upwards of 350,000 pounds with trade, construction, and population increasing all the time. Despite these positive results, I do believe there are limits beyond which the quantity in circulation is harmful to the economy.

Soon after, I won the contract to print the paper money for New Castle with the help of my friend, Mr. Hamilton. As even small things appear great to those with new beginnings, this was another profitable job and a great encouragement, too. Hamilton also helped procure for me the printing of the laws and votes of the government at New Castle. This job stayed with my print shop for as long as I followed the day-to-day operations of the business.

I expanded my business by opening a small stationer's shop. With the help of my friend Brientnal, I drafted and sold a wide variety of standard business forms. I also sold paper, parchment, and an assortment of small books. About this time, a workman from my London days, Mr. Whitemash, showed up at my shop looking for work. I knew his reputation and he proved to be an excellent and diligent worker. I also took an apprentice, the son of Aquila Rose.

I've told you much of these matters using nothing but "I" and "me." I want to clearly state, however, that my partnership with Meredith continued. If I write as though only one person were running the shop, that's because this was the truth of the matter. The entire management of the business lay on my shoulders—but I knew this going in. Meredith could not set type and was not much better at working the press. Worse still, he had gone back to his old drinking habits and was seldom sober. My friends in the Junto lamented my being stuck with him in a partnership. Contrarily, I could see nothing but opportunity.

CHAPTER 31

Setting Up My Own Shop at Last

Nobody ever said starting your own business is easy, and Franklin demonstrates how treacherous it can be to navigate the marketplace. Along the way, he turns away from personal convenience to honor prior commitments. Although cynics might doubt Franklin's good intentions, it's worth noting that he treats Meredith's family very fairly in his reconstruction. He also shows us the importance of initiating difficult conversations. He deserves full credit for successfully dissolving an unequal partnership without using blame and accusations to pressure the other party.

IN BUSINESS YOU NEVER KNOW WHAT'S JUST around the corner, and I would soon run into a frightening new difficulty. As you may recall, Meredith's father agreed to put down all the capital necessary to help us start our print shop. His initial investment of 100 pounds had allowed us to order our equipment, but he still owed another 100 to the merchant to cover the entire bill. Unfortunately, this merchant became impatient for the money and sued us to get it. We paid bail and avoided an immediate judgment. However, it was clear that if we could not pay the other 100 pounds soon, we would surely lose when the matter went to court. This would ruin our business as our equipment would be sold—probably at half its value—to satisfy the debt.

During this stressful time, two of my friends—acting separately with no knowledge of the other's intention and without invitation from me—approached me and offered their assistance. Specifically, each offered to advance me all the money necessary to settle this debt and then buy out my partner. They both told me that Meredith was often seen drunk in the streets and gambling foolishly in the alehouses. Such behavior only served to hurt our credit, despite my own good behavior in public.

Grateful as I was, I told them that I could not accept their offer for help and dissolve the partnership while there remained any chance that the Meredith family might prove capable of fulfilling their part of the agreement. After all, the Merediths had stepped forward to help me at a time when nobody else had, and I felt myself under great obligation to them. As such, my intention was to go forward with them as far as possible. Should they fail in their performance and our partnership disintegrate, only then would I be at liberty to accept help from my friends. Incidentally, these two friends were William Coleman and Robert Grace, and I've always remembered their great kindness.

> POOR RICHARD ONCE SAID, "SELL NOT VIRTUE TO PURCHASE WEALTH, NOR LIBERTY TO PURCHASE POWER."

Time passed and there seemed to be no progress on the matter of the outstanding debt. I delicately approached Meredith and said, "It might be possible that your father is dissatisfied with our partnership and is unwilling to give more money to the two of us where he would give to you alone. If you suspect this is the case, just let me know. I'll let you buy me out and I'll find another business." Meredith then told me that his father was indeed disappointed but also genuinely unable to provide us further financial help. "And," he said, "I don't want to cause him any more stress. I'm simply not fit for this printing business. I was meant to be a farmer and I was foolish to go to the city at 30 years of age and apprentice myself in a new trade."

Meredith went on to tell me that he wished to move to North Carolina as other Welsh people were doing at the time. "Land is cheap there," he said, "and

I can return to farming." He then told me that if I would take over the current debts, return his father's initial investment of 100 pounds, pay a few of his own personal debts, and give him 30 pounds and a new saddle, he would leave the whole of the partnership to me. Needless to say, I agreed to his proposal and contacted my friends immediately.

The new contracts were drawn up and signed within a matter of days. I gave him what he asked and he soon headed off to North Carolina. During the next year, he sent me two long letters from his new lands. These letters contained the best account I had yet seen of the Carolinas regarding the climate, soil, farming conditions, and the like. He had clearly returned to his proper trade. I printed his letters in my newspaper and heard many good comments about them from the readers. Incidentally, I was averse to showing preference to either Coleman or Grace for help in the refinancing. I graciously took half of what I needed from each and went into business in my own name. I subsequently advertised that the partnership with Meredith was dissolved. I was 24 years old at the time.

CHAPTER 32

The Power of a Good Reputation

Franklin deliberately managed his public reputation to maximize his business opportunities with both creditors and customers. This chapter details the early growth of his business and how two of his competitors ruined themselves. At the end of the chapter, he gives us a marvelous guideline for making ethical decisions: you should design your institutions assuming that you may not always be the one in power.

ONE OF MY EARLY GOALS WAS TO PAY OFF the debt I was under for setting up my own shop. I took great pains to establish a good reputation as a businessman because it makes the process of getting credit much easier. I worked hard and I spent no money unnecessarily. I also made sure I avoided any appearance of either laziness or poor money management. I dressed plainly. I never visited places where idle people gathered to drink, gamble, or needlessly amuse themselves. I never went out hunting or fishing as a show of sport or leisure. Of course, a book sometimes drew me away from my work, but that was seldom. Anyway, it's better to be caught reading than gambling.

To demonstrate both my work ethic and that I didn't think too highly of myself, I sometimes brought back the paper I purchased at the stores through the streets in a wheelbarrow. Such activities cemented my local reputation as an industrious, enterprising young man. Because I paid my bills on time, the merchants who imported paper and printing supplies began seeking me out as a customer. Times were good at my print shop. Keimer's credit and profits, in contrast, declined steadily after I opened shop. Ultimately, he was forced to sell his print shop to pay his creditors. He later sailed off to Barbados, where he lived for years in very poor circumstances, which I'll detail soon.

Keimer's apprentice, David Harry, bought his master's materials and set up in his former shop in Philadelphia. I had instructed Harry while I worked at Keimer's place and knew that I now faced a more capable rival who could seriously cut into my business. Thus, I went to him and proposed a partnership, but he scornfully rejected it. In the end, I was thankful that he did so, for he proved to be a poor master of his own shop. He dressed in fancy clothing, lived expensively, and frequently took long vacations. As a result, his debt grew, his shop declined in his absence, and all his customers left him. At this point he packed up his print shop and also sailed off to Barbados where he had the curious privilege of employing his former master, Keimer, as his journeyman. They fought all the time. Needless to say, Harry's debt only grew there, and his creditors ultimately forced the sale of his equipment to pay it off. The person who bought his types in Barbados employed Keimer but died a few years later. Harry returned to Pennsylvania and worked in the country.

I now had no competitor in Philadelphia but Bradford. He was comfortably wealthy at this point and cared little for expanding his business. He was, however, the local postmaster, and everyone assumed this gave him a better opportunity to keep up with the news. As a result, his newspaper remained popular and carried more advertisements than mine—a profitable deal for him. He deliberately put me at yet another disadvantage, using his position as postmaster. He forbade his riders to deliver my newspapers by post even though they would deliver his own newspaper. The public never knew this since I managed to deliver my papers by post anyway by paying the riders on the side. I thought

> **POOR RICHARD ONCE SAID, "DILIGENCE IS THE MOTHER OF GOOD LUCK."**

his behavior so tyrannical that, years later, when I became postmaster, I made sure that any newspaper willing to pay the fee could send their paper through the post.

———◆———

CHAPTER 33

Getting Married

Benjamin Franklin and Deborah Read formed a common-law union in September of 1730, and there is ample evidence that they enjoyed one another's companionship until her death in 1774. They could not enjoy the benefits of a public marriage ceremony owing to problems with her previous marriage, which Franklin explains here. In this chapter he also mentions forthrightly his visiting "prostitutes and other low women." Although he doesn't mention it in his autobiography, a child from one of these unions showed up on the Franklins' doorstep a few months after Deborah moved in. It's a testament to Deborah's character that she took another woman's child and raised him as her own. The identity of the mother remains a mystery to this day. They named him William Franklin, and he would end up opposing his father during the Revolutionary War.

I STILL SHARED THE HOUSE I RENTED WITH THE Godfrey family. From time to time, Mr. Godfrey still ran his glass-making business in part of my shop. The bulk of his time, however, was devoted to his fascination with mathematics. Mrs. Godfrey played matchmaker for me with the daughter of one of her relatives.

She brought this girl and me together as often as possible. Soon enough, I became interested and pursued a courtship. Her parents encouraged the match by frequent invitations to dinner and by letting the two of us spend time together. When it came time to discuss the matter of marriage, Mrs. Godfrey stepped forward to mediate the agreement.

As to a dowry, I told Mrs. Godfrey that I expected a sum large enough to allow me to pay off the remaining debt for my print shop. This would be about 100 pounds—sizable, but certainly manageable. Mrs. Godfrey brought me word that the family could not spare that much money. I then suggested that they might put a mortgage on their home to obtain the funds. It was quiet for a few days but then word came back through Mrs. Godfrey that the parents no longer approved the match. They had spoken with Bradford, and he had told them that the printing business was both unprofitable and costly to maintain. Bradford also pointed out to them that both Keimer and Harry had failed, and that I was sure to follow soon. After this, I received no more invitations for dinner and the daughter was not allowed to leave the house.

I could not tell for sure if they genuinely disapproved of the match or if they feared I would try to steal their daughter. The extreme nature of their behavior led me to believe the latter, and I resented it. I never called at their house again. Some time later, Mrs. Godfrey told me that everything was fine and that I should try to continue the courtship. I remained resolute, however, and had nothing more to do with that family. The Godfreys took this as an insult and decided to move out of my house. After they left, I resolved to take in no more tenants.

This incident had turned my thoughts toward marriage, and I began searching for a wife. To my surprise, most people believed the printing business to be a poor one. Thus, I should not expect any money to accompany my wife unless I chose below everyone's preferences. In the meantime, my passions drove me to frequent relations with prostitutes and other low women. Admittedly, such behavior was both expensive and a risk to health and reputation. I'm grateful that I never caught any diseases.

From time to time I would cross paths with Deborah Read's family. Fond memories remained on both sides from my lodging in their home upon my first arrival to Philadelphia. Her mother began to consult me more and more in the affairs of the family, and I gave help where I could. Deborah's failed marriage with Mr. Rogers had left her rather dejected and she still avoided most company. In all fairness, I had probably contributed to her situation during my absence—and silence—in London and I felt great sympathy toward her. Her mother blamed herself for Deborah's situation since she had prevented our marrying one another prior to my leaving for London and then pressured Deborah into her marriage with Rogers.

In the end, Deborah and I revived our affections for one another. There were some objections to our marrying and I would also put myself at risk. Most people believed the marriage to be invalid since Rogers was said to already have a wife in England prior to his marrying Deborah. But this could not be proven to everyone's satisfaction given the distance. There were reports also of his death, but these were uncertain. If true, however, he had left many debts, which I, as his successor, might be called upon to pay. We ventured forward despite these difficulties and I took her as wife on September 1, 1730. As usual, our worst fears never materialized. Deborah proved to be a great mate and even helped me run my shop. We prospered together and have ever since committed to make the other happy. Thus, I was given the chance to correct as much as possible one of the great mistakes of my youth.

> POOR RICHARD ONCE SAID, "KEEP YOUR EYES WIDE OPEN BEFORE MARRIAGE, HALF-SHUT AFTERWARDS."

CHAPTER 34

Founding the First Library in Philadelphia

A key to getting things done is finding ways to ensure that everyone cooperates. In setting up the first public library in America, Franklin developed a system of contracts, penalties, and privileges to keep the effort going rather than relying on good intentions. Throughout the rest of the autobiography, we'll see Franklin establish private associations that soon become public projects. He'll follow the success of the library with a fire company, a university, and other institutions. It's no surprise that Franklin's first major public project was something that would most likely benefit his business of printing things that people wanted to read.

ONCE MY BUSINESS BECAME STEADY IN PENNSYLVANIA, I could turn my mind to more public matters. For me, one clear problem was that there were no bookstores in any colonial city south of Boston. The printers in New York and Philadelphia sold a few books, mainly almanacs, romantic ballads, and ordinary schoolbooks. Those who wished to read anything beyond these basics had to, like me, order their books from England. The members of the Junto did also, and each of us had a small, private collection.

The club being now well established, we no longer met in a public tavern but rather rented a private room for our Friday evening meetings. One night I proposed that we consolidate our book collections in this room where they could serve as a ready reference during our dialogues. Furthermore, each of us could then borrow the others' books to take home and read. Everyone liked the idea and we managed to keep our collections pooled for some time.

I greatly enjoyed our experimental library and began to envision something on a grander scale. If a dozen friends could do this, why not an entire city? I drew up plans for a public library financed by membership fees. With some legal help, a membership contract was drawn up outlining both the initiation fees and the annual membership dues. It took a lot of work, but I managed to find 50 people interested in reading and wealthy enough to pay the 40-shilling initiation fee and commit to paying 10 shillings a year thereafter for the next 50 years.

Thus, our library began with these meager funds. Books were imported from England and the library was open one day each week for members to check out books. Members were charged double the value of the book if they failed to return the book in a reasonable time. Though small, the library proved to be a huge success and was soon imitated in many other places throughout the colonies. Later, reading became fashionable and libraries began to benefit from the donations of wealthy patrons. As the colonies lacked public amusements like theater or horse racing, many people chose instead to read in their spare time. After a few years, visitors observed that the colonial people were generally more intelligent and more literate than people of the same class in other countries.

Mr. Brockden, the person who helped the original members draw up the first contracts, said something very memorable as we all stood there ready to sign a document commiting funds for the next 50 years. He said to us, "You all are young men, but I predict that none of you will live to see the end of your 50-year commitment." Almost 50 years later, however, a number of us are still alive and may yet outlive his prediction. None of us have paid anything for a number of years, however. The success of the library allowed us to render null and void the original agreements by incorporating the library with a permanent endowment.

> POOR RICHARD ONCE SAID, "THE NOBLEST QUESTION IN THE WORLD IS WHAT GOOD MAY I DO IN IT?"

Let me pass on some valuable lessons I learned during our initial membership drive. Things were difficult at the beginning. I heard many refusals and more excuses as I made the rounds. I soon discovered that it's not wise to present one's self as the champion of any public project that might improve your reputation above that of your neighbor—especially when you need your neighbor's cooperation to make that project a reality. Therefore, I changed my approach.

Steel magnate Andrew Carnegie, a Franklin admirer, used much of his personal fortune to found libraries throughout America. He firmly believed that reading helped one both succeed in business and grow as an individual.

My revised speech framed the library as an idea of a group of people who had asked me to approach people they knew to be lovers of reading and to inform them of the project. This downplayed my role in the matter, and the new approach met with much less resistance. I've used this same approach on several other projects since and can enthusiastically recommend it. Believe me, whatever personal pride you sacrifice upfront will be amply repaid later on. Eventually, somebody more vain than you will move in to take the credit for the success of the project. Astute observers will cut them down, however, and rightfully give you the credit. All you have to do is stay quiet and watch it happen.

CHAPTER 35

Proverbs and Productivity

franklin is perhaps best known for the wise and witty sayings from his series of Poor Richard's Almanacks. *He published the first of these in December 1732 and would continue the series for 25 years. At this point in his story, he's still more than a year away from those publications, but that does not stop him from pointing out the role that wise proverbs have played in his life. He quotes two in this chapter and describes how they applied to his life. By age 24, Franklin's path is clear before him and he begins putting aside his former frugality and concentrating more on style.*

ONCE THE LIBRARY WAS UP AND RUNNING, I set apart an hour or two for study each day. This continued the self-improvement that I began in my younger years and was my education because my father never sent me to college. Reading was the only amusement I allowed myself. I never went to taverns or gambled. I played no games nor attended any of the little parties people held to amuse themselves. I focused all my energies on my print shop, for this was the price of survival and success.

> **POOR RICHARD ONCE SAID, "GOD HELPS THEM THAT HELP THEMSELVES."**

I had many reasons for this focus. I still carried debt for my shop and equipment. I now had children who needed an education. Most of all, I had to compete for business with other established printers. This hard work paid off, however, and my situation grew easier day by day. Also, my habits of frugality continued and I spent no money without good reason.

I attribute these habits to a Biblical proverb my father often told me when I was a boy: "Do you see a man skilled in his work? He will serve before kings; he will not serve before obscure men." I took this proverb to heart and considered productivity as the path to both wealth and honor. Contrary to this Biblical dictum, I never believed I would actually stand before kings. This eventually happened, however. Later in life I would stand before five kings and have had the honor of sitting down to dinner with the King of Denmark.

Speaking of proverbs, there's an old English proverb that says, "He that would thrive, must ask his wife." I was lucky in that the wife I chose was just as hardworking and frugal as I. Deborah happily assisted me every day at the print shop. Among other things, she tended the shop, folded and stitched pamphlets, and purchased old linen rags to resell to the papermakers. Unlike others in our class, we did not employ domestic servants. Our table was plain and simple and our furniture the cheapest that we could find. For years, my breakfast consisted of only bread and milk eaten out of an inexpensive pottery bowl with a pewter spoon. Nor did I care for tea with my breakfast.

But luxury can creep into even the most frugal homes. One morning I sat down for breakfast and found my bread and milk being served to me in a china bowl with a silver spoon. Deborah had secretly bought these for me and they cost an enormous sum by our standards. She had not sought my permission nor did she wish to make apology. She simply said that her husband deserved to eat with a silver spoon and china bowl as much, if not more, than any of his neighbors. In this way, fine china entered our home and, as our wealth increased over the years, our collection grew tremendously.

> Franklin so loved words and writing that late in his life he challenged a friend, Noah Webster, to create a dictionary of the American language. Now, "*Webster's* defines . . ." almost rivals "Poor Richard once said . . ." as an authoritative start to a sentence.

CHAPTER 36

Thoughts on Religion

Franklin lived in a religiously divided society and developed a wonderfully tolerant view of the various religions around him. He affirmed religion as a matter of importance in a nation's life and wanted to make room for diverse practices. More than almost any of the Founding Fathers, his views have affected the interaction of faith and government throughout the history of the United States.

I HAD BEEN RELIGIOUSLY EDUCATED AS A PRESBYTERIAN. However, I found some of their doctrines unintelligible—among them, election, reprobation, and the eternal decrees of God. The doctrines I did understand I doubted so much that I stopped attending church services on Sunday very early in my life. Sunday became my study day. I was never without some religious principles, however. For example, I never doubted the existence of God or that He made the world and governed it by His providence. I believed that our greatest service to God was the doing good to other people. I also believed that our souls were immortal, and that all crime would be punished and all virtue rewarded, either on earth or in the afterlife.

These few beliefs seemed foundational and they appeared in every religious sect in the colonies. These essentials were often mixed with other beliefs that unfortunately served to divide our population and make us unfriendly to one another. In contrast, I believed that religion should inspire and promote moral behavior or publicly confirm its existence when privately practiced. I wished to respect them all and concluded that even the worst of religions had some good effect. I went to great lengths to avoid any conversation that might lessen the good opinion someone had of his own religion. The population of Pennsylvania continued to grow and new places of worship were continually in demand. Almost all were built with voluntary contributions, and I never refused giving money to any sect that cared to ask for my donation.

> POOR RICHARD ONCE SAID, "THE MASTER-PIECE OF MAN, IS TO LIVE TO THE PURPOSE."

Even in my adult years, I rarely attended any public worship service. Nonetheless, I believed that such gatherings—when rightly conducted—were very beneficial for society. Every year I gave a contribution to support the only Presbyterian church and minister we had in Philadelphia. He paid a friendly visit to me from time to time and never failed to tell me that I should attend his services more often. Every so often I gave in to his admonitions and once attended for five consecutive Sundays. Had he been a better preacher I might have given up my Sunday studies and continued attending. His sermons consisted either of peculiar Presbyterian doctrines or rather one-sided theological arguments. I found it all very dry, and he never taught me anything. Since he never inspired us toward or enforced moral living, I was left to assume that he'd rather us all be good Presbyterians than good citizens.

He once got my hopes up by focusing his sermon upon that part of the fourth chapter of Philippians which reads, "Finally, brothers, whatever is true, whatever is noble, whatever is right, whatever is pure, whatever is lovely, whatever is admirable—if anything is excellent or praiseworthy—think about such things." I thought to myself that there was no way that he could avoid the subject of inspiring morality using this text—but he did. He argued that the Apostle Paul wrote this in hopes of our doing five things:

1. Keep the Sabbath Day holy.
2. Read our Bibles every day.
3. Go to church every time there is an assembly

4. Participate in the Holy Communion.

5. Respect God's ministers

All of these might be good things, but they were not the good things that I expected from a sermon on that text. I concluded that his preaching was irrelevant to my daily concerns and I refused to attend any more of their assemblies. Some years before, however, I had composed a short liturgy for my own private use. I called it my "Articles of Belief and Acts of Religion." Thus, I returned to my private religion and went no more to public assemblies. Some might condemn this conduct but I don't care nor do I wish to argue about it. My goal in sharing this is to help people know the facts of my religious behavior, and not to make apology for it.

Successful CEO's have been known to think seriously about religion. Tom Chappell, founder and CEO of Tom's of Maine personal care products, took a break from his company to earn a degree from Harvard Divinity School.

CHAPTER 37

My Plan to Achieve Moral Perfection

This chapter contains what is arguably the centerpiece of the autobiography. It's called "The Art of Virtue" and it was Franklin's grand scheme for achieving moral perfection. It's been both imitated and condemned countless times. Try to avoid your own judgment until reading Franklin's commentary on the undertaking in the following chapter.

AS A REACTION TO THE RELIGIOUS EXPERIENCES previously mentioned, I embarked upon the daring and difficult project of achieving moral perfection. I wanted nothing less than to live without committing any fault at any time. To do so I would have to overcome all the temptations of human nature, custom, and peer pressure. I knew—or thought I knew—what was right and what was wrong and saw no reason why I should not be able to do the one and avoid the other. I soon learned that achieving moral perfection was more difficult than I first imagined.

When I focused my attention on avoiding one fault, I found I was often surprised by another. Passion often proved stronger than reason and bad habits took advantage of any lack of focus or effort on my part. I soon concluded that the mere belief that "we ought to behave better" was not enough to succeed in this undertaking. Stronger measures were necessary. Bad habits must be broken and replaced by good ones if we are to have any hope of being better people. I created the following method to develop such habits.

I had read a great deal about morality and had several versions of what others considered to be the definitive list of moral virtues. Some writers had shorter lists, others had longer lists. Some defined their virtues broadly, while others had more narrow definitions. For example, self-control was limited by some only to eating and drinking; others extended it to all areas of life. For the sake of clarity, I decided to have a larger number of virtues on my list but limit them with narrow definitions. In the end I created a list of 13 moral virtues and gave each a brief definition that captured the principle I hoped to put into practice. Here is my list:

1. *SELF-CONTROL*. Avoid dullness from overeating. Avoid drunkenness from overdrinking.
2. *SILENCE*. Say only those things that benefit others or yourself. Avoid all petty conversation.
3. *ORDER*. Keep all your possessions in their proper place. Give each part of your business its necessary time.
4. *DETERMINATION*. Commit to what you ought to do and always carry out your commitments.
5. *ECONOMY*. Don't waste your money. Let your only expenses be the doing of good to others or yourself.
6. *PRODUCTIVITY*. Don't waste your time. Spend your time on useful matters and refrain from unnecessary activities.
7. *TRUTHFULNESS*. Avoid lies that harm others. Think without prejudice and, if you speak, speak accordingly.
8. *JUSTICE*. Avoid injuring others by your actions, or withholding from them the benefits they deserve.
9. *MODERATION*. Avoid extremes. This applies especially to the holding of grudges against those who have harmed you.
10. *CLEANLINESS*. Keep body, clothes, and living spaces clean at all times.
11. *PEACE*. Don't be overtaken by either small irritants or by the larger troubles that are sure to come.

12. *CHASTITY*. Indulge your sexual appetites for the sake of health and off-spring only. Never indulge to the point of dullness or weakness. Never injure your own or another's peace or reputation.

13. *HUMILITY*. Imitate Jesus and Socrates.

My goal was to make a habit of all of these virtues. To achieve this, I avoided the temptation to conquer them all at once and chose rather to focus on one at a time. Once I had mastered one virtue, then I could proceed to the next until I had mastered the list. Also, as the mastery of some virtues aid in the mastery of others, I arranged the list with the most essential of the virtues near the top. *SELF-CONTROL* was fundamental to any endeavor in which vigilance was needed to break old habits and avoid regular temptations. Once that was mastered, *SILENCE* would come easier and yield its own benefits, too.

SILENCE took second place on my list because I desired to improve my knowledge at the same time as I improved my virtue. This happens by using one's ears more than one's tongue. I had acquired the habit of gossiping, punning, and joking in my conversation, and this made me popular with petty people craving only amusement. This habit needed to be replaced with something better. *ORDER* came next, with the hope that it would help me better manage my time. Wasting time kept me from my studies and this endeavor for moral perfection.

Once habitual, *DETERMINATION* would keep me firmly committed to all my endeavors and to attaining the remaining virtues. *ECONOMY* and *PRODUCTIVITY* could both help me pay off my debts and then achieve wealth and independence. Such a standing would make the practice of *TRUTHFULNESS* and *JUSTICE* easier—I think you probably see the progression at this point.

> **POOR RICHARD ONCE SAID, "WELL DONE IS BETTER THAN WELL SAID."**

Studying Pythagoras and his Golden Verses convinced me that daily attention was necessary to succeed in this great undertaking. So I created a book in which I allotted one page for each of the 13 virtues. On each page I made seven columns—one for each day of the week—and put a letter representing each day at the top of the column. I then made 13 rows across each of these columns and put a letter representing each virtue at the beginning of the line. Thus, I had a matrix in which I could mark—with a black spot—every fault I committed with respect to that virtue. This would be my habit at the end of each day. The pages looked something like this:

SELF-CONTROL
Avoid dullness from overeating. Avoid drunkenness from overdrinking.

	S	M	T	W	T	F	S
S							
S							
O							
D							
E							
P							
T							
J							
M							
C							
P							
C							
H							

I focused on one virtue each week, starting with SELF-CONTROL and working my way down the list. Leaving the other virtues to chance, I took great care not to lose my SELF-CONTROL. At the end of each day, I would tally up offenses for all virtues but hoped to find SELF-CONTROL blank. If I could go the whole week without any transgressions in SELF-CONTROL, that virtue could be considered strengthened and I would try the next week to keep both SELF-CONTROL and SILENCE free of markings. I continued this method for 13 weeks in hopes of mastering all 13 virtues. I conveniently repeated this 13-week cycle exactly four times during the course of a year.

I'd liken this activity to a gardener trying to keep weeds out of his beds. It would exhaust a gardener to eliminate all the weeds in all his beds at one time. Rather, the wise gardener works one bed at a time and, encouraged by his progress, moves on to the next bed to clean out the weeds. Likewise, this system gave me a visual method for tracking the otherwise invisible path of moral progress. I hoped to review my pages frequently and find successive rows of virtues free of markings. I longed for the ultimate thrill of thumbing through a completely clean book after 13 weeks of close, daily examination of my moral character.

The front page of each book I made to track my moral progress carried these three mottos:

> Upon this idea I stand: If there's a Power above us
> (And all nature cries aloud through her works
> that this is so), He surely delights in virtue;
> And that in which He delights must bring happiness.
>
> —ADDISON'S *CATO*

> O, Philosophy, guide of life! O teacher of virtue and corrector of vice.
> One day of virtue is better than an eternity of vice.
>
> —Cicero

> Long life is in Wisdom's right hand; in her left hand are riches and honor.
> Her ways are pleasant ways, and all her paths are peace.
>
> —Proverbs 3:16–17

Believing God to be the fountain of such wisdom, I thought it a good idea to ask for His help in obtaining it. Thus, I composed the following prayer, which was on the next page of my book just before my tables for keeping records.

> O powerful Goodness! Bountiful Father! Merciful Guide!
> Increase in me that wisdom which leads me to my best interest.
> Strengthen my determination to do what wisdom asks of me.
> Accept my good deeds done to your other children as the best response
> I can make in return for the blessings you have first given me.

I also sometimes used a short prayer I found in Thomson's Poems:

> Father of light and life, you are the Supreme Good!
> Teach me what is good; teach me Thyself!
> Save me from foolishness, pride, and vice,
> And all petty pursuits. Fill my soul

With knowledge, conscious peace, and pure virtue;
Sacred, substantial, never-fading bliss!

My third virtue, ORDER, required that each part of my business should be given its necessary time. Thus, one page of this book featured the following method to help me organize the 24 hours of each day:

THE MORNING	5 A.M.	Rise, wash, and address Powerful Goodness!
Question: What good shall I do this day?	6	Contrive day's business and take the resolution of the day.
	7	Prosecute the present study and breakfast.
	8	
	9	Work
	10	
	11	
NOON	12	Read or examine my accounts, and dine.
	1 P.M.	
	2	
	3	Work
	4	
	5	
EVENING	6	Put things in their places.
Question: What good have I done this day?	7	Supper. music, diversion, or conversation.
	8	Examination of the day.
	9	
	10	
	11	
	12	
NIGHT	1 A.M.	Sleep
	2	
	3	
	4	

Individuals can have codes of values as well as companies. The Dwyer Group, one of America's leading franchise companies, lives its code of values every day. Part of their code requires, "speaking calmly and respectfully without profanity or sarcasm."

So, that was the entirety of my plan, and I followed it for some time (with a few breaks along the way). I was shocked to discover that I had more faults than I ever imagined, and I also had the pleasure of watching them decrease. I only made one copy of my record book when I started, and the pages began to fall apart as I scraped the marks of my transgressions off the pages to begin my program anew each cycle. After a while, I transferred the entire project to a more permanent book with pages made of ivory. I permanently stained a red ink ledger into the ivory pages, giving me the chance to record my faults with a lead pencil. The black marks from the pencil were easily removed with a wet sponge, leaving the ledger intact for another round. I followed this program for many years, but its practice gradually decreased to only one cycle per year. Ultimately, I abandoned it altogether as I began traveling abroad and being occupied with a variety of national affairs.

CHAPTER 38

Reflections on the Pursuit of Moral Perfection

So, now you've read the plan. Here's the reality—and a wise reality it is.

I FOUND IT HARDEST TO PUT INTO PRACTICE the virtue of ORDER. In theory, a person should have control of his time; but in practice, this proved difficult for me as master of my own shop. Although my subordinates in the shop might be able to succeed here, I was forced to mix and mingle with the world and would often have to do so on the world's terms. Some of my most important customers would only receive me at the most inconvenient hours. ORDER with regard to my possessions and papers also proved more difficult than expected to practice. I had not sought much ORDER for my things up to this point in my life. Furthermore, I never worried about not finding what I needed since I had a great memory. I found myself becoming more and more frustrated in the attempt to bring ORDER to my life. I considered giving up the attempt and being content with a faulty character in this area.

Then I thought of my neighbor, a blacksmith, who sold an axe to a man one day. This customer told my neighbor that he wished to have the entire head of the axe as shiny as the cutting edge. Knowing this to require a great deal of work, my neighbor agreed to shine the entire surface of the head for the man if he would work at turning the grinding stone. The customer began turning the wheel and the blacksmith had to press the entire face of the axe to the wheel to grind it and shine it. The man had to work quite hard to keep the wheel turning once the blacksmith applied the pressure. The customer grew more and more weary and stopped turning the wheel to check on the progress more and more frequently. After a while, he stopped turning and said he would take the axe as it was. "No," the blacksmith insisted, "keep turning the wheel! The axe head is still spotted and we'll have a shiny head before the day's ended!"

"Possibly," replied the worn-out customer. "But I've decided I like spotted axes best." And such is the case with many people who begin difficult endeavors like achieving moral perfection. It's nearly impossible to break all bad habits and replace them with good habits, so I gave myself a break and concluded that "a spotted axe was best" in this endeavor. Also, a nagging voice in my mind kept suggesting to me that the pursuit of moral perfection might be, in and of itself, contrary to good morals and good sense. Not only might I look ridiculous if people found out about this, but a perfect moral character could be more of a liability than an asset as others might begin to envy and then hate the way you acted. Thus, I concluded, a wise person allows himself a few faults so as to be tolerable company.

> POOR RICHARD ONCE SAID, "HOW FEW THERE ARE WHO HAVE COURAGE ENOUGH TO OWN THEIR FAULTS, OR RESOLUTION ENOUGH TO MEND THEM!"

In the end, I found *ORDER* impossible to implement in my life. Now that I'm old and my memory has grown poor, I wish I had practiced more of it in my youth. So now it's clear that I never achieved the moral perfection I had been so determined to acquire. I never even got close. Nonetheless, I was definitely a better and happier person for making the effort. I liken it to working to improve one's penmanship. Although one may never write perfectly formed letters, one's writing is almost always improved by the effort.

I'd like everyone who reads this book to know that this one self-improvement program, with God's blessing, contributed more to the quality and happiness of my life than anything else I tried. I'm 79 years old as I write this and I can say that if God in His Providence should see fit to reverse my fortunes, the happiness I've known up to this point will help me carry on through whatever suffering might come. Let me say a bit more about how the pursuit of each of these virtues—however flawed that pursuit may have been— contributed to the quality of my life.

SELF-CONTROL gave me the long and healthy life I have enjoyed thus far and I still have a healthy body to carry me some ways yet. *PRODUCTIVITY* and *ECONOMY* helped me avoid trouble in my early years and soon after helped me become independently wealthy. I believe these two virtues also motivated me toward greater learning, and this made me both a better citizen and gave me a reputation among the educated people of my day. My commitment to *TRUTHFULNESS* and *JUSTICE* helped me gain the confidence of my country and the great work it asked me to undertake on its behalf. The combination of the pursuit of all 13 virtues— again, however mixed the final result—gave me a tranquil demeanor and cheerfulness in conversation that even young children find agreeable. Once again, I heartily recommend this undertaking to anyone who reads this book.

Though my program was not completely free of religion—I did pray, after all—no part of it reflected the distinctive beliefs of any particular religious sect. I intentionally hoped to avoid this, for I believe the program gave great results and could be useful to people from a variety of religions. Being a printer and publisher, I knew I'd probably publish it one day, and I made sure that there was nothing in it that would bias any of the current religious sects against it.

My ultimate plan was to publish the program with a little more commentary about each virtue. I'd explain the benefits of having each virtue as well as the problems that come from its absence. I would have called the book *The Art of Virtue* because it could have given the reader usable tools for living a more virtuous life rather than merely telling the reader "Be a better person!" and then giving them no help as to doing this. I liken the latter to the Biblical warning given in James 2:15–16 to those who tell naked and hungry people to "be warmed and filled" but do nothing to help them find clothes or food.

But it so happened that I never was able to publish this document, despite my intentions to the contrary. I did, from time to time, drop bits and pieces of it into some of my other writings (like *Poor Richard's Almanac*), but the demands of my business life and later my public service kept me from spending the necessary time to draw up the program properly for publication. Thus, what I've given the reader here is incomplete (in my mind) but, I hope, enough to catch a glimpse of the greater project.

Let me restate something I've alluded to earlier in this writing: wrongdoing is not harmful to yourself and others because it's forbidden; it's forbidden because it's harmful. As such, it's in everybody's best interest to live a virtuous life if they want to be happy and successful. This is the way the world works. The young people reading this should take special note: nothing will make a person's fortune like simple goodness and honesty. This holds whether you own your own business or you work for someone else. Good people are in short supply, and you won't stay unemployed for long.

CHAPTER 39

Additional Thoughts on Humility

Franklin's original list contained only 12 virtues. Later, a close acquaintance suggested that he add a 13th virtue to his program: humility. Franklin agreed, and now shares his thoughts on how the habit of humility helped him lead a more successful life. To his credit, Franklin models the new virtue by listening to the counsel of well-meaning friends.

MY LIST ORIGINALLY CONTAINED ONLY 12 virtues until a Quaker friend confided in me that I was generally thought to be arrogant. He completely convinced me of my arrogance by citing several examples during conversation. He showed me where I had not been content with being right in past conversations but could be overbearing, even haughty. As a result of his comment, I determined to cure myself of my arrogance by adding HUMILITY to my list of virtues along with a carefully chosen definition of the word.

At first, I could not boast of much success in being humble, but I did have a good deal of success in appearing to others to be humble. I made it a rule not to give voice to any disagreement I had to the opinions of others, nor would I voice the certainty of my own opinions, regardless of the strength of my conviction. Recalling the rules of our Junto, I even refused to use any word or expression—like "certainly" or "without a doubt"—that suggested I had a fixed opinion about a matter. In place of these words, I substituted phrases such as "As I see it . . ." "Now this is only my opinion . . ." or "It appears to me at present . . . ."

If somebody in conversation said something I thought wrong or unfounded, I would deny myself the immediate pleasure of correcting him or showing him the absurdity of his ideas. Rather, I would begin my response by acknowledging that his opinion might be right in certain cases or circumstances, but appeared to me under the present circumstances to have some problems. I soon discovered that this change in my conversational habits was for the better, and my conversations took on a much more pleasant tone. Proposing my opinions in a humble fashion assured them a more attentive and less defensive listener. I suffered less embarrassment when I was genuinely found to be in the wrong. Better still, when I was in the right I discovered that my humility more readily motivated others to give up their mistakes and join my side.

> POOR RICHARD ONCE SAID, "HUMILITY MAKES GREAT MEN TWICE HONOURABLE."

At first I really struggled with this kind of humility in my conversations. It gradually became easier, however, and developed into a natural habit. This habit is so strong I can now say that no one has heard a dogmatic opinion escape my lips for almost 50 years. I now believe that this habit of humility is second only to my habit of personal integrity in helping me promote my ideas among other individuals. If the truth be known, I am a poor public speaker, completely lacking in eloquence, and I often stumble through my choice of words. Yet as a result of my habit of humility, I often find my proposals succeeding where they might otherwise have failed, and I have gone on to establish numerous public institutions and reform a number of others in need of repair.

Pride is probably the most difficult of our natural passions to tame. You can disguise it, fight it, suppress it, or degrade it over and over again, but it comes back at you on many occasions as strongly as ever. Pride is so strong that you can probably spot it in these very autobiographical writings of mine, so look no further than this: for even if I could convince myself that I had overcome my pride, I should probably be proud of my humility.

CHAPTER 40

Some Counsel on Grand Undertakings

Franklin was no stranger to grand undertakings—just consider his role as one of the Founding Fathers of the United States. Here he shares with us one of the more grand undertakings that he abandoned along his way to building a nation. By way of example, he demonstrates that big projects require a good bit of study, a well-developed plan, and a motivated champion. This chapter closes with what I find to be some of his most encouraging remarks.

I'LL RETURN SOON TO A DISCUSSION OF HOW I grew my business in Philadelphia and beyond, but first I want to mention another project aimed at moral improvement at the cultural level rather than the individual level. It began as a paper I wrote about two years before I developed *The Art of Virtue*. After reading a number of history books, I made the following observations:

1. Political parties of like-minded individuals both cause and affect the great events of the world—its wars, revolutions, and the like.

2. Each of these parties acts in its own best interest, or at least what it believes to be its interest at the time.

3. Every party differs in its primary interests, and this causes a great deal of conflict.

4. Every person in these political parties has a personal interest that may or may not coincide with the party's interest.

5. As soon as a party achieves its general interest, each member begins to pursue his private interest. As these will vary greatly across all members, there will be a great deal of conflict and more division.

6. Few people in public affairs act with the good of their country in mind, whatever they might say to the contrary. Even though their pretensions can bring genuine good to their country, this happens by accident. No one in public affairs acts out of general benevolence, but each believes that what he wants and what the country wants is often the same thing.

7. As such, almost no one in public affairs ever acts with the good of humankind in mind.

8. Therefore, I see an opportunity for beginning a new political party: the United Party for Virtue. Such a party would gather the good and virtuous people of all nations together to be governed by good and virtuous laws. Good and virtuous people will be more willing to follow good and virtuous laws than conventional people are willing to follow conventional laws.

9. Thus, whoever is qualified to do so and attempts this venture will certainly please God and meet with success.

I kept this project in mind for many years, always hoping to make it happen should the opportunity arise. As I waited for the necessary break in my work, I jotted down some thoughts along the way. One piece I found many years later contains what looks to be a creed I wrote, which includes what I thought at the time to be the core essentials of every known religion. I was also careful in what I wrote so as not to offend anyone who practiced a religion. The goal, after all, is to get them to embrace my ideas. The creed reads as follows:

1. There is one God who made all things.
2. He governs the world by His Providence.
3. He should be worshipped by words of adoration, prayer, and thanksgiving.
4. The most acceptable service to God is the doing of good to other men.

5. The soul is immortal.

6. God will both reward virtue and punish wrongdoing, either in this life or the one hereafter.

When I wrote this, I was of the opinion that this new religion should be begun and spread only among young single men. Each person who joins the sect should not only have to declare his agreement to the creed but also should have already gone through at least one 13-week cycle of my previously mentioned method for promoting virtue. The sect, I believed, should be kept secret until it became quite large so as to avoid having unsavory individuals wanting to join for the wrong reasons.

> POOR RICHARD ONCE SAID, "HE THAT CAN HAVE PATIENCE, CAN HAVE WHAT HE WILL."

As such, the members of the sect should carefully consider their friends and reveal the scheme to the intelligent, well-adjusted people among them. With an invitation to join, each member should also offer their friends advice, help, and support in promoting one another's mutual interests in business and in life. I thought the whole endeavor should be known as "The Society of the Free and Easy." We were "free" because the habitual practice of virtue freed us from the tyranny of wrongdoing. Particularly, by the regular practice of *PRODUCTIVITY* and *ECONOMY*, we would all be free from debt, which is its own kind of slavery, and could more "easily" accomplish what we desired.

I can't recall anything else about this undertaking except that I once communicated it to two of my friends who, in turn, enthusiastically adopted it. My busy life never allowed me to pursue it further, however. To this day I've not tried to pick it back up, and I confess that I no longer have the strength for such a grand project. I still believe the project could be successful if undertaken, however, and it might make a great number of good citizens along the way. So if you like what you see, give it a try and don't be discouraged. I have always thought that one man of even moderate abilities can create great changes and leave a powerful legacy if he has a good plan, stays focused on it, and dedicates his life to making that plan a reality.

CHAPTER 41

Poor Richard's Almanac Introduced

Franklin created many alter egos for his writing projects and you've already met two of them: Silence Dogood and the "Busy Body." For his best-selling series of almanacs, Franklin created the character of "Poor Richard" Saunders. The almanacs of Franklin's day contained a variety of information, including calendars, municipal events, medical advice, philosophy, poetry, and the like. As a bonus, Franklin included a number of wise and witty sayings in the margins of his almanacs, and these are some of his most memorable phrases. Sometimes, it's what's in the little spaces that makes a product special. Ironically, Franklin may have sparked more cultural transformation with this one business product than with the grand plans he shared with us in the previous chapter.

IN LATE 1732, I PUBLISHED MY FIRST Poor Richard's Almanac under the name of Richard Saunders. My goal was to make the books both entertaining and useful. The concept worked, and I continued publishing the books for almost 25 years. The series sold nearly 10,000 copies a year, and I reaped considerable profit as a result. Once I realized the popularity of the book, I decided to use it as a way to cultivate virtue among its readers—especially among the farmers and working class who rarely attended school or bought any book other than an almanac. Thus, I filled in every empty space I could find in the book's calendars with wise and memorable sayings. Most of these sayings focused on the benefits of *PRODUCTIVITY* and *ECONOMY* as the way to wealth. Others captured basic moral principles in easy-to-remember images. For example, moral philosophers teach that needy, desperate people are often more motivated to act dishonestly. To help reach the intended audience, I captured this teaching in the proverb, "It's hard for an empty sack to stand upright."

These proverbs, which captured the wisdom of many ages and cultures, proved very popular with readers. I inserted as many as I could into the preface to the 1757 *Almanac* in the form of a speech given by a wise old man to a group of people in the marketplace. The collected wisdom showcased in this piece packed a real punch and proved wildly popular all over

> POOR RICHARD ONCE SAID, "SEARCH OTHERS FOR THEIR VIRTUES, THY SELF FOR THEY VICES."

the world. It was reprinted in newspapers all over the European continent and two French translations were made of the document. In Britain, it was reproduced on a large poster and hung in homes and public spaces. Members of the clergy bought hundreds of reprints to pass out among the poor in their parishes. The wealthy property owners did the same among their poor tenants. The speech's focus on *ECONOMY* discouraged the purchase of foreign-made luxuries. As such, its circulation was widely believed to result in a decrease in such spending and a growth in the money supply throughout Pennsylvania.

I could also use my newspaper for such educational purposes. I often reprinted essays about morality from the *Spectator* and other sources. In early 1735, I began publishing my own work in the newspaper once it had survived a round of critique in the Junto. Examples of such writing included a Socratic dialogue leading to the conclusion that, regardless of his abilities, an unrepentant wrongdoer could never be considered a good, sensible man in the end. I also published an essay of my own on the topic of self-denial. It contended that virtue is not secure until its practice becomes a daily habit and all bad inclinations eliminated.

As publisher of my own newspaper, I made it a rule to never publish anything libelous or news of personal scandal. Unfortunately, nowadays publishers disregard this rule and our country is worse off because of it. Whenever people brought such items to my newspaper, they regularly pointed to "freedom of the press" as they pleaded their case with me. Some even offered to pay for the space, claiming that my newspaper was like a stagecoach and anyone willing to pay could have a seat. I responded to such people that I would be happy to print their piece separately if they so desired, and the author could distribute as many copies as he wished to purchase. I would not, however, use my newspaper to help circulate his particular grievance. My subscribers trusted me to furnish them a paper containing useful and entertaining information, and it was against the integrity of our relationship to fill the paper with private arguments which did not concern them.

Too many of the printers in Pennsylvania publish false accusations to gratify the petty grievances of any paying "stagecoach passenger" without giving it a second thought. Such libel not only blackens the reputations of our finest citizens but fuels arguments that sometimes lead to duels. Other publishers rush to print poorly written and defamatory essays about the governments of neighboring countries or national allies. Such acts abuse the power of the press and can often result in vicious retaliations. I mention this for the benefit of young printers who might be inclined to go against their better judgment when tempted with money. If nothing else, my story demonstrates that standing firm in moments like that won't ruin you in the long term—though you might think such at the time.

CHAPTER 42

Franchising Across the Continent

More than most, Franklin understood the power of well-designed con-
tracts. In fact, the agreement he crafts in this chapter is a precursor to
the franchise system that has grown numerous businesses in the United
States, such as McDonald's. This chapter is also among Franklin's most
pro-woman writings. For more of his views on the role of women in soci-
ety, interested readers should study his "The Speech of Miss Polly Baker."

IN 1733, I HELPED SET UP ONE OF MY JOURNEYMEN in his own print shop in
Charleston, South Carolina. The city was in need of a good printer at the time,
so we agreed to a partnership and I sent him on his way. Our agreement was
that I would pay one-third of the expenses and receive one-third of the profits of the
business in return. He was an honest and educated fellow but a poor accountant.
Every so often he would send me some money, but I could never get any good information from him about the financial state of our partnership. When he died, his
widow took over the business.

She had been born and reared in the Netherlands where (so I've heard) they teach accounting to all women as part of their education. She not only sent me a decent financial summary of his past business dealings but continued to provide perfect accounting statements on a regular basis. She proved an excellent manager of the busi-

> POOR RICHARD ONCE SAID, "THERE'S MORE OLD DRUNKARDS THAN OLD DOCTORS."

ness and a capable mother as well. When the original partnership agreement expired, she had enough money saved to purchase the business outright from me and hand it over to her son.

I include this story to point out that a good business education for women will serve them better in the event of their becoming widowed than the currently fashionable educations women receive in either music or dancing. Furthermore, a good business education will help them more easily spot devious men, who regularly con widows out of their money. There is no reason a widow cannot continue a profitable business operation until her sons come of age to take it over. Everyone benefits from a good education, and everyone suffers from the lack of one—especially women.

With a chain of print shops, newspapers, and control of the postal system, Franklin established one of the first media empires in America. This puts him in the same league as William Randolph Hearst, Ted Turner, and Rupert Murdoch.

CHAPTER 43

Learning Languages

In this chapter Franklin shows us that incentive is everything when trying to improve oneself. He demonstrates that learning can be fun and, along the way, makes some suggestions to language teachers. Take note of how much Franklin valued usefulness over complexity. When choosing between traditional academic rigor and practicality, Franklin almost always went for the practical.

I BEGAN STUDYING LANGUAGES IN 1733 AND SOON mastered French well enough to easily read books written in that language. I tackled Italian next, inspired by a rather curious learning incentive. A friend was studying Italian at the same time I was and occasionally coaxed me into a game of chess. I soon discovered that our chess games were significantly infringing upon my study time, and I refused to play another game with him unless he agreed to the following. Whoever won the game would impose a task upon the other, which had to be performed upon their honor by our next meeting. The catch was that this demand was to be given—from memory or from notes—in Italian. Being pretty evenly matched at chess, we eventually beat one another into mastering Italian.

> POOR RICHARD ONCE SAID, "THE ANCIENTS TELL US WHAT IS BEST; BUT WE MUST LEARN OF THE MODERNS WHAT IS FITTEST."

Afterwards, I studied enough Spanish to also read their books.

As you may recall, I had enjoyed only one year of instruction at a Latin school and that was when I was very young. Furthermore, I had neglected the language entirely after that time. When I began to study French, Italian, and Spanish, however, I was surprised to find how much Latin I'd retained when I perused a Latin Testament one day. This motivated me once again to study Latin, and I found it quite easy to do on the heels of learning the other languages.

This made me think that maybe we have our method of language instruction backwards. Supposedly, we must first master Latin before we can master the modern languages that are derived from it. My experience suggests to me that it might work the other way around. It is true that if you can somehow get to the top of a staircase without using any steps, then you'll certainly find it easier going down. However, it's true also that if you actually use the lower stairs to reach the upper stairs, you will more easily make it to the top.

Therefore, I have this advice for those who oversee the education of our youth. Why start with Latin? It's not only the most difficult to master, but people can struggle with it for years and then find it to be almost useless. Students can even become bitter about the time they lost studying it. We might better begin with a modern language they might actually use, like French, and then gradually work backwards to the ancient languages. This method would probably take the same amount of time as the study of Latin, and the students might eventually discover the wonder of ancient languages like Latin. If not, at least they are left with one or two languages that they might retain through regular use in modern life.

Franklin not only traveled to Europe on several occasions throughout his life, he also studied other languages. These experiences proved instrumental in his business success. As our world continues to globalize, more and more business students are studying a foreign language and taking advantage of study-abroad experiences before they graduate from college.

CHAPTER 44

Fighting the Good Fight

Few things mattered more to Franklin than making a positive contribution to society. In this chapter he comes to the aid of a Presbyterian minister who runs afoul of his church. It's worth noting that even though Franklin is so displeased with the outcome that he once again stops attending church services, he shows balance and humility by continuing to support the church with monetary donations.

IN ABOUT 1734, A NEW PRESBYTERIAN PREACHER arrived in Philadelphia from Ireland. His name was Hemphill. He delivered his sermons in a strong voice and, apparently, without any notes whatsoever. A number of people from different religious sects, including myself, went to admire him, and I returned to church once more to attend his sermons. I liked him because he didn't preach about doctrine but rather about how to become a better person and increase your good works. Those who considered themselves orthodox Presbyterians opposed him, however, and went to the church synod in hopes of having him silenced.

> **POOR RICHARD ONCE SAID, "BLESSED IS HE THAT EXPECTS NOTHING, FOR HE SHALL NEVER BE DISAPPOINTED."**

I rushed to his defense and organized his admirers. We fought hard, and our hopes for success grew weekly. Both sides wrote a great deal during the struggle, and soon I discovered that our talented preacher was a poor writer. In an effort to help, I wrote several pamphlets and even one article in my newspaper using his name. The article can be found in the paper's April 1735 archives, but all copies of the pamphlets—as is generally the case with such things—have apparently disappeared from the face of the earth.

Our struggle took a bad turn when one of our adversaries came to hear Hemphill preach and thought his sermon sounded too familiar. After some research, he produced a document from a British magazine proving that our Hemphill had lifted part of his sermon from one preached by a Dr. James Foster. Many of his supporters scattered after this and we were then quickly defeated in the synod. I stuck by him, though, as I would rather him preach good sermons composed by others than preach bad sermons of his own creation (as was the practice of most of the preachers of our day). He later confessed to me that he never preached a sermon of his own composing. Rather, his memory was so good that he could repeat sermons word for word after only one reading. Eventually he left in search of a friendlier home and I left the congregation. I never again attended its assemblies but did continue my support of its ministers for many years.

———◆———

CHAPTER 45

Family Matters

Franklin's humanity shines forth once again in these two vignettes about his family. One benefit in writing about one's life is that one can some-times point with satisfaction to situations in which peace is made after seemingly irreconcilable conflicts. Here Franklin finally makes peace with his brother James, his harsh former master.

IT HAD NOW BEEN TEN YEARS SINCE MY LAST VISIT to Boston, and my business was on a firm enough footing to allow me an extended leave. I set out to visit my family and soon discovered that I had almost waited too long. I stopped in Newport along the way to visit my brother James. He had long since established his printing business in Rhode Island and his health was declining fast. We had put to rest our former differences with the passing of time and our meeting was very warm. Telling me that his death was near, he asked me to care for his ten-year-old son after his death and to bring the boy up in the printing business. I agreed, and kept my promise when the day came. I sent the child to school for a few years before I allowed him to work in the shop, though. James's widow managed the print shop

> **POOR RICHARD ONCE SAID, "LOVE, AND BE LOV'D."**

until he was old enough to take over. At that time I presented him with a variety of new types, as those his father used were worn out. Thus, I made amends with my brother and repaid in full the services of which I had deprived him when I ran away.

I lost a child of my own to smallpox in 1736. He was a fine boy of four years old. We chose not to vaccinate him against the disease because the vaccination itself sometimes takes the child's life. I've long regretted this decision and it grieves me to this day. I mention this for the sake of parents who might be tempted to make the same decision we made, believing that they might never forgive themselves if the vaccination should take their child's life. I can tell you from experience that your regret will be the same either way, and that you should err on the side of caution and vaccinate your children whenever possible.

———⟢⟡⟣———

CHAPTER 46

Update on the Junto

Although he does so at several points in the autobiography, Franklin shows us here that there are multiple solutions to any given problem. Rather than debate the point of adding new members to the Junto or not, Franklin turns the conversation in a new direction with an unexpected solution. He shows us by example that there is often a third way . . . and probably a fourth, too. In addition, he demonstrates the power of self-replicating patterns of influence.

THE JUNTO HAD NEVER STOPPED MEETING DURING all these years, and everyone involved agreed that it was one of their most beneficial activities. Several in the club wanted to enlarge the membership by inviting friends to join. We could not, however, achieve this without violating the founding agreement to limit the size of our club to 12 members. From the beginning we had also agreed to keep our club secret and, with one or two exceptions, we had succeeded. Such secrecy helped us avoid requests for membership from undesirable people whom we also might find difficult to refuse.

I strongly opposed adding to our number and, rather than endlessly argue the point, I proposed an alternative solution. I suggested that each member of the Junto should take the lead in starting a new club with the same rules as ours. Also, this new club should not know about the existence of the Junto. One benefit of this growth strategy, I contended, was that it allowed more people to enjoy the benefits of our Junto than would otherwise be the case were we merely to add new members. This strategy would also allow us to learn quickly the opinions of the general population by coordinating the queries asked in these new clubs each week, and then having the members of the Junto report on the matter when we met on Friday evenings. The Junto then might have the opportunity to influence the opinions in these new clubs and promote both our own interests and the common good.

> POOR RICHARD ONCE SAID, "ONE MAN MAY BE MORE CUNNING THAN ANOTHER, BUT NOT MORE CUNNING THAN EVERY BODY ELSE."

The project was approved and each of us took the lead in forming a new club. The project met with mixed results. Only 5 or 6 clubs, out of 12 attempts, took on a life of their own, but these showed us the great power of the basic idea. These new clubs named themselves—the Vine, the Union, the Band, being examples—and the new members benefited from the meetings. Beyond this, these new clubs gave those of us in the Junto a great deal of amusement, information, and, on a few occasions, taught us a thing or two. Later, I'll discuss how we used these new clubs to influence public opinion on several occasions.

CHAPTER 47

Advice on Changing Someone's Opinion of You

How do you change somebody's bad opinion of you? Franklin suggests that you don't try to do it all at once but rather by small degrees. Here he shares the story of how he maintained a civil relationship with someone who would rather be his enemy. His actions demonstrate the importance of the Consistency Principle: Once somebody has done a small favor for you, chances are that they will do a larger favor for you later. There is indeed power in helping others, but there is also power in letting others help you first.

ONE OF MY FIRST BIG BREAKS CAME WHEN I was chosen to be clerk of the General Assembly in 1736. Incidentally, I was chosen this first time without any opposition whatsoever. The next year I had to be reconfirmed, as did the members of the General Assembly. During the reconfirmation process, a newly elected member of the Assembly gave a long speech opposing me and favoring another candidate. I was nonetheless chosen again in 1737 and undertook the office with even greater confidence in my qualifications. The pay associated with the position was nice, but the opportunity it provided was even better. I now inter-acted with the members of the General Assembly on a regular basis, and this helped me secure the contract for printing the official business of the province, including the votes, the laws, and the paper currency.

> **POOR RICHARD ONCE SAID, "THERE IS NO LITTLE ENEMY."**

Let me say something about this new Assembly member who appeared to dislike me. He was an educated gentleman with a good-sized fortune and talents capable of gaining him great political influence over time—and this indeed hap-pened. I thought it a bad idea to try to change his opinion of me by catering to him in a subservient fashion. Rather, I took a different route that would better preserve both our dignities. I had heard that in his personal library he had a copy of a rare and interesting book. I wrote him a note, asking whether he would do me the favor of lending me the book for a few days so that I might glance through it. He sent it imme-diately, and I returned it within a week with another note, expressing my appre-ciation.

The next time we met in the Assembly, he spoke to me—something he had never before done—and he did so with great civility. From then on, we helped one another and our friendship continued until his death. This incident illus-trates the truth of a proverb I had previously learned which states, "Expect more help from those who have once done you a favor than from those for whom you have done a favor." It also demonstrates the wisdom of taking action to remove conflict, as most other roads will tend toward escalation.

CHAPTER 48

How to Displease Your Superiors

Now Clerk of the Assembly, Franklin continues to move toward the center of influence in Philadelphia by becoming Deputy Postmaster of Philadelphia. As with being Clerk, it wasn't the pay that mattered in this job but the opportunities it afforded for Franklin's printing-related businesses. The story of how Andrew Bradford fumbled away his job as Deputy Postmaster to his competitor is a warning about how we are often our own worst enemies. Franklin shows us that if people trust you with their money, they'll trust you with other things as well.

IN 1737, THE POSTMASTER-GENERAL FOR AMERICA was Colonel Spotswood, the recently retired governor of Virginia. For the past few years, he had grown more and more irritated with his deputy postmaster of Philadelphia, my competitor, Bradford. It seems as though Bradford no longer cared to send him accounting reports and so Colonel Spotswood took the commission from Bradford and offered it to me. Needless to say, I jumped on the opportunity. Once again, the pay was small but the opportunity was great. I could now deliver my newspaper without paying Bradford's riders on the side to do it.

> **POOR RICHARD ONCE SAID, "IF YOU WOULD BE REVENG'D OF YOUR ENEMY, GOVERN YOURSELF."**

As a result, my subscription rate grew and subsequently increased my advertising income. My delivery costs dropped without the extra payments, so my income from the paper increased considerably. Bradford's newspaper declined somewhat and this gave me a bit of satisfaction as I had vowed earlier not to retaliate against him for refusing to deliver my newspapers. In the end, Bradford suffered from neglecting both his newspaper and his superior. I share this story as a lesson for all who manage the affairs of others. Nothing gives your superiors more confidence in your abilities than communicating financial information in an accurate and timely manner. And few acts gain their disfavor quicker than the failure to do such.

CHAPTER 49

Building a Better Community

One of the most important themes to emerge from Franklin's autobiography is that great entrepreneurs are also great citizens. Here Franklin turns his attention to making life in Philadelphia better and safer for the average citizen. Notice how he leverages his business acumen in reforming civic affairs. That is, good pay often gets better results than volunteerism, and qualified, interested individuals keep watch better than disinterested ones. He began making reforms at the local level and, as you know, ended up succeeding with some truly "revolutionary" reforms at the national level.

FROM TIME TO TIME, I TURNED MY MIND TO community affairs and tried to make some small contribution. I'd rather try small projects as large projects are more likely to fail. After a bit of observation, I decided that I could substantially improve our city's night watch. The constables from each of the city's wards managed the watch and here's how it was supposed to work. The constable notified a number of households each night that they would be helping him that

> POOR RICHARD ONCE SAID, "MINE IS BETTER THAN OURS."

night as he made his rounds. For the price of six shillings a year, a household could be excused from such duties, however, and the constable would then use this money to hire substitute helpers. In reality, six shillings a year from households wishing to be exempt was far more than was necessary to hire the needed help, and this made the office of constable a place of profit. Worse yet, for the promise of a little drink, some constables hired rather disreputable substitutes who volunteers from respectable households disliked as partners in making the rounds.

With this kind of help, the night watch was often populated by drunks and the rounds were generally neglected. It was an invitation for trouble and an unnecessary security risk. I wrote up my ideas for reform and presented them to the Junto for sharpening. The focal point of my argument was the unfairness of the six-shilling exemption tax collected by the constables. The poor widow on a fixed income paid the same amount for public protection as the wealthiest merchant, even though the value of their respective property holdings differed significantly.

I presented the Junto with a plan for a more effective watch. It centered on funding the constable's office with a tax proportionate to the value of one's property, rather than a flat tax. My plan also recommended paying qualified individuals to staff the night watch continually rather than rely on volunteers and other even less motivated individuals. The idea was approved by the Junto and subsequently taken up for discussion by the other clubs started by our members. In this manner we began to prepare the minds of the people for the

Personal security has long been the basis of great business ideas. From the founding of the Pinkerton National Detective Agency in 1850 to the proliferation of car alarms, home security systems, and network security companies, entrepreneurs find that it sometimes pays to be on the defensive.

necessary change. Within a few years, the night watch was a matter of regular public discussion and the members of our clubs were in positions of influence. A law was then passed making this plan a reality.

CHAPTER 50

Founding the First Fire Department

It's hard for us to believe that Franklin's Philadelphia was a world without fire departments, police departments, or a standing army—at least until he started working on the matter. In the previous chapter, he reformed the night watch. In this chapter, he founds Philadelphia's first fire company—the Union Fire Company. In the absence of a fire department, if your house caught fire, whether by lightning, arson, or accident, you lost everything, as did many of your neighbors. Unlike some people of his day, Franklin did not believe that fires were a form of divine punishment but could be controlled and prevented if one studied the matter, took action, and shared information with others. Franklin may have been prouder of his founding of the Philadelphia fire companies than just about any other of his accomplishments. As with many of his undertakings, the fire companies began as privately funded initiatives and, later, evolved into publicly funded institutions.

ALONG WITH MY ATTEMPT TO IMPROVE THE NIGHT watch, I also floated a paper with the Junto regarding house fires. Specifically, I sought to explain what caused them and how one could prevent such fires in the future. The Junto

> **POOR RICHARD ONCE SAID, "WITHOUT JUSTICE, COURAGE IS WEAK."**

loved the paper and I eventually published the ideas in my newspaper. I took the lead in forming a fire company that could act to extinguish fires at a moment's notice and work to save whatever property it could. I soon had thirty individuals who signed an agreement specifying our two main obligations to one another. First, each member was required to keep at the ready a certain number of strong leather buckets to be brought to every fire. Second, we agreed to meet once a month to talk about recent fires and share information about ways to prevent and extinguish them.

The usefulness of the company was soon obvious to everyone in the community, and we soon advised others in how to form their own fire companies, because we did not think it wise to just make ours larger. Soon enough, just about every property owner in the city belonged to one of these fire companies. Though it has now been 50 years, my original fire company, the Union Fire Company, still stands at the ready, though all the founding members but me and one other have died.

Along with founding the first fire department, Franklin also organized the Philadelphia Contributionship—the nation's oldest insurance company and one of the first cooperatives. Other well-known cooperatives include Land 'O Lakes, Sunkist, Sunmaid, dozens of rural electric cooperatives, and the VHA cooperative in the health care industry.

The small fines that were paid over the years by members who missed regular meetings were used to purchase equipment such as mobile water pumps, hooks, ladders, and other useful equipment beyond our original bucket brigade. I now wonder whether there is a city in the world better equipped to fight fires than Philadelphia. In fact, since these companies began forming 50 years ago, the city has never lost by fire more than one or two houses at a time. Furthermore, the flames have often been extinguished in burning homes before more than half of the house was consumed.

CHAPTER 51

The Reverend
George Whitefield

Franklin devotes more pages in his autobiography to the Reverend George Whitefield than to any other character. This may be because Franklin knew Whitefield to be a master communicator and champion of humanitarian projects. His support of Whitefield also indicates that Franklin truly believed in a marketplace for ideas. That is, all people should have a chance to persuade their fellow citizens to the rightness of their views in the public arena. As Franklin notes, his tolerance even extended to religions outside of Christianity, such as Islam. At the end of this chapter, observe how Franklin competently employs the Reciprocity Principle. That is, when he does a favor for Whitefield, he expects to have the favor returned in this life rather than in an afterlife—and he lets Whitefield know this.

IN 1739 A GENUINE CELEBRITY ARRIVED IN our city: The Reverend George Whitefield from Ireland. At first, some of our churches welcomed him to their pulpits but the clergy soon objected and Whitefield was forced to preach in the fields—a situation to which he had grown accustomed in England. He attracted huge crowds from all religious traditions. I attended his sermons, too, but only to observe their influence on his listeners. Despite regular assurances from Whitefield that they were little better than animals, the crowds loved him. During his visit, a genuine religious revival broke out in our region and one could not walk through the streets without hearing psalms being sung nearby.

Whitefield possessed a clear, loud voice and near-perfect articulation. This improved his preaching effectiveness because he could be heard and understood from a great distance. His audiences helped too, as they always remained perfectly silent. He preached one evening from the top of the courthouse steps where Market Street and Second Street intersect. The crowds of people listening to his sermon extended a long distance down both streets. Being near the back of the crowd on Market Street, I decided to walk backwards down the street toward the river to determine just how far one could hear his voice. To my surprise, I found that his voice remained clear all the way to Front Street, where some noise began to distort it. I then imagined a semicircle in which this distance was the radius, and calculated how many people could stand within it if they were each allotted two square feet of space. My answer was 30,000 people. Although there was not so large a number on this day because of the buildings, this calculation gave credibility to some newspaper accounts of his having preached to 25,000 people in the fields of England.

It's always inconvenient to assemble in the open air owing to uncertainties with the weather. So someone proposed building a great hall, which could give visiting preachers like Whitefield a pulpit from which to speak. Funds were collected in short order and, in the spirit of revival, a structure—100 feet long and 70 feet wide—was quickly erected. The building was controlled by trustees who dedicated it to the use of preachers of any and all persuasions who might like their chance to speak to the people of Philadelphia. I hope that even if the Grand Mufti of Constantinople were to send someone to teach us about Islam, there would be a podium at the ready.

I listened to Whitefield preach as often as possible and soon learned to distinguish between his new sermons and those he had preached for a long time during the course of his travels. His delivery of these more familiar sermons was incredibly good. Every point of emphasis, every raising and lowering of the voice, was so perfectly placed and executed that—regardless of the sermon's topic—listening to him speak was as pleasurable as listening to someone perform a good piece of music. I concluded that it's better to be a traveling preacher like Whitefield than a preacher with a fixed pulpit and a regular congregation. Preachers assigned to congregations cannot reap the benefits of repetition and therefore must work harder both to create more sermons and deliver them better the first time.

Reverend Whitefield left us soon thereafter to preach throughout the rest of the colonies and on into Georgia. Georgia had just begun to be settled and it was a unique undertaking. Some may not know that Georgia was settled by the near-criminal element of our society—bankrupt shopkeepers, people taken from the jails, and the like. These people could barely survive in civilized surroundings and the Georgian wilderness proved difficult for many of them to master. As a result, many of the settlers died, leaving behind a large number of orphans. Whitefield was deeply moved by the sight of these children and determined to build an orphanage in the area where these children might receive care and education. He championed this cause in his sermons as he made his way back north and collected a great deal of money. He was, after all, powerfully eloquent and could open the hearts and the purses of those who heard him, myself included.

I thought the project a fine undertaking and recommended one slight change. At the time, Georgia was wilderness and had neither available materials nor skilled workmen. Whitefield planned to send such from Philadelphia at great expense. I suggested that it might be better to build the orphanage here in Philadelphia and bring the children northward. He was fixed in his mind, however, and rejected my counsel. I therefore decided to withhold my contribution from his project.

> Faith and religion can be big business, too. The well-respected Billy Graham Evangelistic Association has more than $300 million in assets and publishes an annual report. The Willow Creek Community Church near Chicago was the subject of a famous Harvard Business School case in the 1990's.

The next year, I again attended one of his sermons in our great public hall. Toward the end, it became clear that he was going to ask for a donation. I again resolved in my mind that he would get nothing from me. I had in my pocket at the time a handful of copper money, three or four silver dollars, and five *pistoles* in gold. As he proceeded I softened a bit and decided to contribute the coppers. Listening further, I felt ashamed of giving only the coppers and put in the silver the next time the offering was taken. His conclusion was so strong that I emptied the rest of my pocket, gold and all, into the collection.

Another member of the Junto was also at this sermon. He and I were of the same opinion about the orphanage in Georgia and he had the foresight to empty his pockets before he left home, lest he be tempted to contribute. Toward the end of the sermon, he too felt a powerful urge to contribute to the project. He found his neighbor standing nearby and asked to borrow some money for just this purpose. His neighbor, however, was the only person in the building immune to Whitefield's influence. He replied, "At any other time, my friend, I would lend you money without hesitation. But tonight I will not, since you seem to not be thinking properly."

I had the pleasure of getting to know the Reverend Whitefield better after being hired to print his sermons and journals. Some of Whitefield's enemies raised doubts about whether he would build an orphanage with these funds or pad his own pocket. I found Whitefield to be a man of great integrity and can now say 45 years later that his conduct was perfectly honest with these funds and with other matters. Such an endorsement ought to carry a bit of weight since we shared no religious connection. We remained civil and sincere acquaintances until his death.

Here are a few more stories that will shed some light on our relationship. Once when he returned to Boston he sent word to me that he would soon travel to Philadelphia. His previous host, Mr. Benezet, had moved to another town and Whitefield asked my advice concerning where to lodge during his stay. I responded, "You are familiar with my house and if you don't mind its simplicity, you are most welcome to stay here." He liked the idea and replied that my reward was certain if I had extended such hospitality for the sake of Jesus Christ. I quickly shot back, "Please don't be mistaken. I extend this invitation not for Christ's sake but for your sake." When receiving favors, Godly men have a custom of shifting the burden of obligation from their own shoulders and placing it in heaven. In my response, my goal was to weaken his attempt and remind him of his earthly obligation to repay this hospitality.

> **POOR RICHARD ONCE SAID, "GIFTS MUCH EXPECTED, ARE PAID, NOT GIVEN."**

Despite his strengths as a preacher, his published writings gave him great trouble from time to time. When preaching, one can get away with an unguarded expression or an unsupportable position from time to time, or at least one can qualify what one said after the fact when questioned. The spoken word might pass away but the written word remains. Thus, his critics violently attacked his writings and with such effectiveness as to decrease his number of disciples. I'm of the opinion that he would have been better off if he had never published anything. Had he not, he probably would have left behind a large following after his death and his reputation would have continued to improve. In the absence of the written word, his followers could have fancied him as wonderful as their imaginations would allow without having critics point out his published flaws.

The last time I saw Reverend Whitefield was during a visit to London. He consulted me about his now established Bethesda Orphanage and his plans of converting it into a college. He often told me that he prayed for my conversion to Christianity. He never had the satisfaction of knowing that this prayer was answered, however.

CHAPTER 52

Franklin the Inventor

In addition to being an entrepreneur, a statesman, and a scientist, Franklin was a distinguished inventor. Among other things, he invented the lightning rod, bifocal glasses, and what became known as the Franklin stove. This stove enabled people to heat their homes with less fuel and less risk of damage from fire. Franklin wrote this account in 1788, knowing that wood was becoming scarce in his part of the world. Not long after, entire colonies would be deforested in the search for fire-wood. As a result, any invention that saved fuel was of benefit to everybody. This chapter counters the notions of those who wish to portray Franklin unfairly as a greedy capitalist.

IN 1742, I INVENTED A STOVE THAT HEATED A ROOM better than a fireplace. The design of the stove was key to its fuel efficiency. I gave a model of the stove to my friend Robert Grace, who cast plates for the stove in his iron furnace. He discovered, to his delight, that the stoves he made began to sell. To increase the demand for the stove I published a pamphlet of my own entitled "An Account of the Recently Invented Pennsylvania Fireplaces." This pamphlet detailed the stove's design and operation, explained the comparative advantage of the stove to other methods of warming a room, and provided a defense against possible objections that might be made against the stove.

The pamphlet indeed increased demand. Governor Thomas was so impressed with the design of the stove that he offered me patent protection for the exclusive manufacture of the stoves for a period of time. I declined his offer, however, and based my decision on this principle: Every day we benefit from the inventions of other people throughout history. We should therefore be honored to return the favor by freely and generously giving back an invention of our own once in a while.

And what is the result of such a principled stance? In this particular instance, a hardware merchant in London plagiarized my pamphlet, made a small design change in my stove (which actually hurt its operation), and received a patent for it in England. My friends told me that he made a small fortune on the sale of the stoves there. From time to time other people also benefited from my inventions, though not everyone made a fortune doing so. I never disputed any of them, however. I hate disputes and have no desire to profit by my inventions. My reward is this: That the use of my stove in this and other colonies in America has allowed and will continue to allow the users to cut much less wood to fuel their fires than ever before.

> POOR RICHARD ONCE SAID, "TRICKS AND TREACHERY ARE THE PRACTICE OF FOOLS, THAT HAVE NOT WIT ENOUGH TO BE HONEST."

CHAPTER 53

On Partnerships

Always wanting to help the first-time entrepreneur, Franklin offers valuable advice in this chapter about managing business partnerships. He also extends the franchising concept he introduced in Chapter 42. Along the way, he gives us a brief update on his own businesses.

SINCE MY PARTNERSHIP IN CAROLINA HAD succeeded so well, I decided to set up a few more and give some of my best workers the chance to run their own shops. As before, I designed a profit-sharing contract in which I furnished the seed capital with the goal of the workers purchasing full ownership back from me at the end of six years. Most of them achieved this goal and thereby lifted both themselves and their families to better circumstances.

Partnerships are usually difficult and often end in conflict, so I'm happy to report that all of these worked well and ended on friendly terms. I attribute this success to our clearly defining the roles and expectations of each partner at the very beginning in our contract. With such clarity, there is little to dispute. I heartily recommend this approach to all who enter into partnerships. Business partners may indeed have

> POOR RICHARD ONCE SAID, "HE THAT SELLS UPON TRUST, LOSES MANY FRIENDS, AND ALWAYS WANTS MONEY."

admiration for and confidence in one another at the beginning of the partnership, but it rarely lasts. Petty jealousies arise along the way and they begin to disgust one another. Or each perceives that the other is carrying less than his fair share of the business's burden. Eventually, the friendship breaks up and often a lawsuit or worse results.

My business now had a life of its own, and every day my circumstances became easier. My newspaper had become very profitable and was for a time the only newspaper in this and the neighboring regions. In fact, a quarter of my subscribers were from outside of Philadelphia. I learned the truth of the age-old observation that, "After earning one's first 100 pounds, it's easier to get the second 100." Money grows and reproduces itself.

———⟫●⟪———

Stock options are a form of contingent contracts in that they reward employee-owners for working to grow the wealth of the firm. Both Wal-Mart and Microsoft used generous stock options during their early years to reward growth. Many employees became millionaires as a result.

—⟶❯❮⟵—

CHAPTER 54

Proposing a College, Establishing a Militia

In 1743 Franklin wrote, "The first drudgery of settling [the] new colonies is now pretty well over, and there are many in every province in circumstances that set them at ease, and afford leisure to cultivate the finer arts, and improve the common stock of knowledge." Franklin had hoped to improve the common stock of knowledge by founding a college. Instead, he "settles" for starting the American Philosophical Society— the country's first learned society. He'll return to the college idea again in a few chapters. In starting a militia, Franklin shows once again that not all great efforts require the hand of government. He deftly leapfrogs a breakdown in government and shows that there are many paths to organization. And take note of how Franklin convinces people of the need for change before trying to affect change.

I LOVED LIVING AND WORKING IN PENNSYLVANIA BUT found there was always to be room for improvement. Two things, in particular, began to concern me. First, we had no militia in the state; we were entirely defenseless. Second, we had no college and the youth had no means of completing their educations.

Thus, in 1743 I drew up plans for establishing a college. The Reverend Mr. Peters was not working at the time, and I shared these plans with him in hopes that he would see fit to manage such an institution. He was certainly qualified to do so but was considering doing work with the Penn family, the proprietaries of Pennsylvania Colony. These projects came through for him, and he declined to help with my project. I didn't know anyone else as well qualified as he, so I decided to wait a while rather than go forward with the wrong person leading the effort. I didn't establish the college in 1744, but I did propose and establish the American Philosophical Society.

Regarding defense, Spain had been fighting a long war against Great Britain and had now been joined in the fight by France. This put the colonies in great danger, and enemy warships were spotted from time to time on our waters. Our governor at the time, Mr. George Thomas, had worked long and hard with the pacifist Quaker Assembly to pass a militia law and thus improve the security of the province. The law was thwarted at every turn, however, and never passed. In the absence of a legislative solution to the problem, I took it as a challenge to raise a purely voluntary militia.

To get this started, I wrote and published a pamphlet, enti- tled *Plain Truth,* in which I clearly documented our region's defenselessness. The pamphlet called for an organized defense and promised to propose such publicly and call for volunteers in a matter of days. The pamphlet spread quickly and I set about drafting a militia contract with a few friends. As promised, I scheduled a meeting within a few days for all interested citizens in the large hall built during Whitefield's

> POOR RICHARD ONCE SAID, "HE THAT WAITS UPON FORTUNE IS NEVER SURE OF DINNER."

stay. The hall was quite full, but I was ready. I had printed a large number of copies of the contract for the volunteer militia and had pens and ink at the ready all throughout the hall. I spoke more about the need for a volunteer militia and then explained the contract in detail. When we passed the contracts around the room, they were signed immediately and without objection.

When the meeting ended, we counted 1,200 signed contracts. People carried copies of the contract with them after the meeting and circulated them around the region. In the end, we had 10,000 signatures. Everyone who signed up for the militia set about buying guns and ammunition. They then self-organized into companies and regiments and chose their own officers. These groups met once a week to drill themselves and practice their military discipline. The women of the province pooled their funds, too, and presented each company with silk flags masterfully decorated with unique designs and mottos (which I happily supplied).

CHAPTER 55

The Politics of Fortification

In this chapter Franklin provides some inspiration on handling political opposition. Unlike today, there were few taxes available to finance public projects. They were funded instead with lotteries—a very common practice in those days. Similar to what we call a "raffle" today, lotteries offered tickets at low, fixed prices, promising a large payout to a randomly selected winner on a certain date. The organizers of the lottery funded their project with whatever was left over. Before this chapter ends, Franklin shows us how to navigate some rather treacherous political waters and how to hold fast to our principles without creating enemies unnecessarily.

THE OFFICERS OF THE PHILADELPHIA REGIMENT met together and chose me to be their colonel. Knowing I'd make a terrible military officer, I declined their offer and recommended in my place a more qualified fellow, Thomas Lawrence. They agreed to my recommendation and he was appointed. Now that a militia was organized, our next task was to build a fortified wall below the city and obtain some cannons for it. I proposed a public lottery to help with the costs of building the fortification. The lottery sold well and we soon erected a fortified wall framed with logs and filled with dirt. We used some of the funds to purchase old cannons from Boston, but there were not enough to defend the site properly. We wrote to England asking for more cannons. We also asked the Penn family for help but, honestly, expected help from neither that quarter nor from the Crown.

Meanwhile, Colonel Lawrence, myself, and a few other men traveled to New York in hopes of borrowing cannon from Governor Clinton. He refused our initial request and then made the mistake of inviting us to dinner with him and his council that evening. Their custom was to enjoy a great deal of Madeira wine as they dined, and we took advantage of his softening to secure a promise of six cannons. More bottles of wine led to more cannons and we improved our score to 10 and, finally, to 18 cannons—and he was happy to give them after all the Madeira. It was excellent artillery—large 18-pounders, complete with carriages for transport. We moved them immediately to our fortification, where the volunteer militia kept a regular guard while the war lasted. I took my turn there among the rest as a soldier on the watch.

POOR RICHARD ONCE SAID, "TAKE COUNSEL IN WINE, BUT RESOLVE AFTERWARDS IN WATER."

Governor Thomas of Pennsylvania and his council were very impressed with my leadership in this undertaking, and they began consulting me on a regular basis. This only improved the effectiveness of our volunteer militia and secured additional resources. I recommended to the governor that we should soon proclaim a fast to seek the help and favor of the religious community. They embraced the idea but there had never been a publicly proclaimed fast in the province, and the governor's secretary had no idea as to how to write such a proclamation. Having grown up in Boston, where fasting was an annual event, I knew how to frame such a proclamation and undertook this, too, for the governor. The proclamation called all to repentance and asked God's divine blessing upon our defensive endeavors. It also invited all who heard it to help in the common defense by joining our volunteer militia. It was printed and distributed to clergy throughout the province. Britain made peace with Spain and France before the proclamation reached maximum distribution. Had that not happened, I believe we would have benefited from large numbers of volunteers from every one of the religious sects—excepting, of course, the pacifist Quakers.

Speaking of the Quakers, some of my friends began to suggest that my public involvement in these military affairs would offend the Quaker community and cause me to lose my position as clerk of the General Assembly, where they held a large majority. Rumors seemed to spread, and ultimately I was approached with an interesting proposition by a politically well-connected gentleman. He informed me that a deal had already been made behind closed doors to have him replace me as clerk to the Assembly in the next election. He thus advised me, in goodwill, that I should resign now and save my reputation rather than suffer the humiliation of being voted out.

I responded to him that I had once heard of a politician who made it a rule never to ask for a public office and also never to refuse one offered to him. "I like his idea," I said, "and will draw upon it in this situation with one small addition: I shall never ask, never refuse, and never resign an office. If they wish to give my office to another, they must take it from me properly. I will not, by resigning the office, too soon lose the privilege of retaliating against my adversaries." Afterward, I heard no more of such rumors and was unanimously chosen once again as clerk to the Assembly after the next election.

I may indeed have offended some Quakers in the Assembly by my public involvement in these military affairs. After all, when the Assembly failed to pass the necessary legislation, my solution of the volunteer militia solved the problem nicely and gained the favor of the governor and his council. They all probably looked a bit foolish in the end. As they would look even more foolish by punishing me for my success, maybe their best hope was having me step aside without a fight. Obviously, I did not do so and took care not to give them another reason by my own foolish behavior.

CHAPTER 56

On Managing Dilemmas

This chapter contains one of the longest and most complicated stories in the autobiography. Here Franklin continues to steer between the difficult politics of the Quaker pacifists and the dangerous realities of colonial security. Fortunately, he had already realized that what people say in public and what they're willing to settle for in private are often two different things. The key to reaching agreement is to find a legitimate way to help the opposing parties save face. In the end, a shrewd minority party helped a powerful majority party do just that.

DESPITE THEIR PACIFIST STANCE, I HAD EVERY reason to believe that the defense of the region was not disagreeable to the Quakers, provided only that they were not required to participate in it. Upon private investigation, I found the majority of them in favor of defensive war despite their public stances against offensive wars. Many pamphlets were being published on the matter of the war and more than a few were by Quakers. Those Quakers writing in favor of a defensive war were very persuasive among the younger Quakers.

I think I discovered this while doing business with some Quakers regarding our fire company. Prior to doing it through the militia, we hoped to use the fire company as the vehicle through which a lottery would be held to raise funds for the building of our fortifications. We needed to sell enough tickets to raise 60 pounds for this project. According to the company's rules, no money could be allocated to a project the same week it was proposed. Thus, we had to wait a week to vote on the matter.

The fire company consisted of 30 members, 22 of whom were Quakers. The other eight came to the next week's meeting a bit early, having no idea if we could garner the eight additional votes it would take to secure a majority. Only one Quaker, James Morris, showed up to oppose the measure and expressed deep sorrow as our meeting began that such a horrible project had even been proposed. Despite being the only one present at the time, he claimed that all the Quakers in the company were against it, and the fire company would surely break apart if we were to press the matter further. The eight of us responded that we knew we were in the minority and would willingly submit to the rule of the majority rather than fracture the company. It came time to put the matter to a vote of the company and, still being the only Quaker present, Mr. Morris asked if we might wait a bit longer before we voted, being certain that the others who opposed the proposition would soon arrive.

As we debated this point, a waiter came in to tell me that two gentlemen wished to speak with me in the room below ours. I went down and found, to my surprise, two of our Quaker members. These gentlemen informed me that eight of their number had assembled in a nearby tavern and stood ready to vote in favor of the matter, if necessary. However, they wished to cast a public vote only if absolutely necessary because doing so in this situation could cause them trouble in their Quaker communities. I returned upstairs certain of a 16-vote majority and gladly agreed to Mr. Morris's request to wait another hour. He was delighted to hear this but grew increasingly disappointed as the hour passed and not one more Quaker showed up for the vote. We carried the resolution by a vote of eight to one.

Of the 21 missing Quakers, eight were ready to vote with us and 13, by their absence, suggested that they had no desire to vote in opposition. Those absent were all members in good standing who regularly attended our meetings and had plenty of notice about this one. I concluded that while Quakers often conform to a pacifist stance in public, only about 1 in 20 might actually believe this enough to follow it in private.

I had mentioned earlier that a few of the Quakers had written pamphlets declaring support for defensive war. The honorable and educated Mr. James Logan wrote one of the best of these pamphlets. Furthermore, he purchased 60 pounds' worth of lottery tickets and told us to use any of his prize money to help build the fortification. He once shared with me this curious story about that well-known Quaker, William Penn, and how he dealt with the matter of self-defense. Logan had traveled to America from England with Penn and served as his personal secretary. A war was being waged at the time and their ship was chased by an armed vessel. Fearing the enemy, the captain took defensive meas-ures and told Penn and his large group of Quakers that he did not expect them to participate in the defense of the vessel.

> POOR RICHARD ONCE SAID, "MEN & MELONS ARE HARD TO KNOW."

The Quakers all went below deck except for Logan, who stayed above and was given a gun. To everyone's relief, the armed vessel proved to be friendly and no fighting occurred. When Logan went below deck to share the news with his fel-low Quakers, Penn rebuked him harshly for taking up arms and going against Quaker doctrine, especially given that the captain himself had excepted them from this service. Being in no mood for a public reprimand, Logan was furious and shot back, "You have more authority over me than the captain. Why didn't you order me to go below deck? It seems to me that you'll take all the protection you can get when you think your own life is in danger."

From my years of service to the Quaker-dominated Assembly I can add other related stories. The Quakers suffered particular embarrassments when the Crown requested the Assembly to provide funds for military purposes. This put them in quite a dilemma: would they choose to go against their pacifist princi-ples, or would they choose to offend the Crown? They always found a way to save face, however, by disguising their compliance with the Crown's requests while, at the same time, giving every appearance of faithfulness to their pacifist principles. The most common of such evasions was allocating the public funds using the phrase "for the king's use" and then never asking how the money was used—knowing full well, of course, that it would go to military purposes.

Sometimes the demand would not come directly from the Crown and they would come up with other phrases to disguise their compliance. Once, a fortress in New England requested funds from the Pennsylvania Assembly for the purchase of gunpowder. Governor Thomas supported the request and urged its passage through the Assembly, contending that our citizens benefited from the protections provided by that fort. The Quakers, of course, were averse to allocating the funds because funds for gunpowder support military activities. Nonetheless, they passed a bill of aid for New England, allocating 3,000 pounds, given directly to Governor Thomas, for the purchase of "bread, flour, wheat, or other grain." Some of the governor's council advised the governor not to accept the funds in hopes of embarrassing the Quakers by exposing their hypocrisy. He wisely replied, "I'll take this money and speak nothing of it because I clearly understand their true intention. They use the phrase 'other grain' to refer to gunpowder." Governor Thomas then purchased 3,000 pounds' worth of gunpowder to send to New England and heard no objection whatsoever from the Quakers.

I kept this story in mind as I created contingency plans in the fire company in case our proposed lottery to finance the fortification failed to pass. I told one of the members in favor of the lottery, "If we fail, let us propose that we purchase a 'fire-engine' with the money—the common name for a movable water pump. Everything I have heard suggests that the Quakers might not object to that and it could pass. Then we'll nominate ourselves as the committee to complete the purchase and we will buy a big cannon, which could also be called a 'fire engine' since it produces so much fire." This member agreed to the contingency plan and said, "You've learned well during your service in the Assembly. This sounds like the same ploy they used when they agreed to purchase 'wheat or other grain.'" We never had need of this contingency plan despite its creativity.

The Quakers suffered frequent trouble and embarrassment as a result of their pacifist stance. I believe that they should never have published it and circulated it so broadly. Once something like that is published, it becomes increasingly difficult to change one's mind, even if one wished to do so. In more recent times, the number of Quakers in public office has been steadily declining because they have chosen to give up their power rather than their principle.

I found the conduct of the Dunker sect much better in contrast. I made friends with one of their founders, Michael Welfare, soon after the sect became established. He told me that the Dunkers were often persecuted by other sects and falsely accused of all manner of horrible practices and beliefs of which they were not even familiar. I consoled him that new sects had suffered such abuse since time began, and I advised him that one of the quickest ways to put a stop to such trouble would be to publish their principles and practices for all to read.

He said that this had already been suggested among their sect but they had decided against doing it. "When we were first called to gather with one another," he told me, "God helped us realize the value of some of the doctrines we had long believed were wrong, and that other doctrines were true that we had once condemned. Ever since, God has improved our beliefs, bit by bit. Our truth continues to grow and our errors decrease. We have no idea when God's perfecting of us will end, so we're reluctant to print out a formal confession of faith. Once we do, we suspect we'll feel so committed to it that we might not allow God to continue improving us. And think of those who will follow in the footsteps of our faith. They might even fancy the views of their elders and founders to be something sacred, from which they should never turn."

As every other religious sect I know supposes itself to be in possession of the truth, the Dunkers' example might just be the only instance of modesty in the historical record. This reminds me of how life is often like being in foggy weather. You can clearly see the terrain that is near you and you often think that those who are further from you are stuck in the fog. Although things might appear clear to you, those at a distance fancy that they are the ones in the clear and that you are stuck in the fog.

CHAPTER 57

Founding the University of Pennsylvania

Every great institution you see around you had a simple beginning. What are you planning to start? In this chapter, Franklin finally gets his learning academy started, and it's now known as the University of Pennsylvania. Note the pattern that has emerged regarding Franklin's involvement in public projects: First, check with the Junto. Second, build up some interest via the press. Third, champion it as the proposal of a "public-spirited" person rather than yourself. Fourth, carefully design the governance structures. And, fifth, turn it over to the public for greater funding and longevity.

BRITAIN, FRANCE, AND SPAIN HAD NOW MADE peace with one another and the matter of the militia and fortification came to an end. I decided to try once again to establish a college or academy in Pennsylvania so our youth could properly complete their education. I drafted a few friends from the Junto to help me design the project and we published a pamphlet entitled "Proposals Relating to the Education of Youth in Pennsylvania." I distributed this free of charge to the wealthiest inhabitants of our province. After they had had some time to read and reflect on the pamphlet, I approached them about giving funds to the project to be paid in yearly installments for a period of five years. By spreading the payments across five years, I suspected that their total contributions might be larger than the amount of a lump sum at the beginning. I was right about this, and we ultimately raised 5,000 pounds.

Once again, I circulated this proposal not under my own name but under the guise of "some public-spirited gentleman." This was in keeping with my usual rule of not presenting my own self as the creator of any scheme for the benefit of the public. Those who supported the project chose 24 individuals from the list of donors to act as trustees. These trustees then appointed me and the current Attorney General, Mr. Francis, to draw up a constitution to govern the academy. Once this was completed and signed by all, we rented a building, hired some teachers, and the school opened within a couple of years of our beginnings.

Entrepreneurs and businesspeople have founded and endowed universities throughout American history. Western Auto Company founder George Pepperdine started Pepperdine University. Commodore Cornelius Vanderbilt endowed his namesake university in 1873. More recently, successful businesspeople have endowed individual business schools rather than universities.

Our enrollment increased so quickly that the building soon proved too small and we began to look around for a well-located piece of real estate upon which to build a larger structure. Providence threw another solution our way and it took the form of the aforementioned building erected to accommodate those who wished to hear the Reverend Whitefield speak. With a few alterations, it would suit our purposes quite well. Here's the story of how we obtained it.

You may recall that the trustees who governed the use of this building were drawn from a wide variety of religious sects, with great care taken to balance the power among them lest any should dominate and shut out the opinions and program of the others. Furthermore, only one person from each religious sect (Baptist, Presbyterian, Moravian, etc.) was allowed as a trustee. The Moravian trustee had the habit of regularly offending his colleagues and when he died, the remaining trustees decided that they would have no more of that sect among them.

Thus, their new problem: How could they appoint a new trustee without giving some particular sect two seats on the board? Several names had been put forward but not agreed upon as they did not solve the above problem. Ultimately, somebody mentioned my name, stating that I was merely an honest man of no sect whatsoever. My profile seemed to please them all, and I was chosen as a trustee. Once on the board I learned that the initial passion for the building had long since faded and the current trustees were having trouble meeting the building's operating expenses. Being a member of two boards, I attempted to negotiate an agreement between the two to save one from further embarrassment and help the other meet its growth needs.

> POOR RICHARD ONCE SAID, "BEING IGNORANT IS NOT SO MUCH A SHAME, AS BEING UNWILLING TO LEARN."

We reached the following agreement. The ownership of the building would be turned over to the trustees of the academy, who would clear all debts the building currently carried. The academy would also forevermore keep open in the building a large hall to be used by traveling preachers as needed. Furthermore, the academy would maintain a free school for the education of the children of poor families. The academy then divided this great hall into several stories and divided each story into a variety of rooms. With the purchase of some nearby real estate, the location soon fit our purposes and the students and teachers moved to their new setting.

As hoped, the trustees of the academy were later incorporated by a charter from the governor. This increased the operating budget for the school through contributions from both Britain and additional land grants from the Penn family. The Assembly made additional contributions and this led to the establishment of the current University of Pennsylvania. I have continued as a trustee of this institution for nearly forty years now and had the great pleasure of watching the youth of Pennsylvania further their educations. Nearly all have improved their abilities and have gone on to distinguish themselves in both private undertakings and public service to their country.

CHAPTER 58

Retiring from My Business

Franklin retired from his business a few weeks before his 42nd birthday and began a life of public service. He did not know it at the time, but this would be the halfway point of his life. Once he stepped aside from his business, the public wisely pushed him forward into leadership positions. His first few offices are detailed in this chapter and are precursors of things to come in the third section of this book. Though Franklin retired from the daily management of his printing business, he remained an owner and benefited from the profits. He maintained this arrangement for another 18 years until he ultimately sold the business to his partner, David Hall.

THE WORK REQUIRED TO BUILD THE NEW ACADEMY fell upon my shoulders, and I gladly accepted the burden of purchasing the materials, contracting with the workers, and overseeing the construction. I enjoyed the work because I had now retired from my printing business and turned its daily operation over to someone else. My partner was David Hall. He had worked for me for the last four years and we shared common values and a common work ethic. He oversaw

> **POOR RICHARD ONCE SAID, "INDUSTRY, PERSEVERANCE, & FRUGALITY, MAKE FORTUNE YIELD."**

the entire operation and regularly paid me my share of the profits. Our partnership lasted for 18 years and was a great success for both of us.

Once retired from the daily affairs of my business and secure in my lifestyle with a modest income, I dedicated some time to scientific studies and, truth be told, a few amusements. My first attempt in this regard was the study of electricity. Dr. Spence had come from England to lecture about the subject, and with great enthusiasm I purchased all his equipment. The public, however, had different plans. They now considered me a man of leisure and enlisted my time, talent, and dedication in matters of government and beyond.

Governor Thomas put me on the Peace Commission to work with both friends and foes through diplomatic means. The corporation that oversaw Philadelphia appointed me as a city councilman and then asked me to be alderman of the group. Last, the citizens of the city chose me as their representative in the Assembly. I best liked joining the Assembly. I could now take part in the debates where as clerk I could only sit there. Actually, as clerk for the Assembly I often entertained myself during some long and boring debates by playing mathematical games like the now popular magic squares and circles. As a member of the Assembly, I could put these aside and hopefully do some good for the community. My son, William, took my place as clerk when I moved to join the Assembly.

I also attempted the office of the justice of the peace for a while. I held court and sat on the bench to hear disputes but found that I needed more familiarity with the laws than I possessed at the time. I eventually withdrew from this position, claiming my obligation to attend to my greater duties as a member of the Assembly. Although I write as though all these promotions were nothing but an inconvenience, I must honestly say that I was flattered by all this attention. Given my humble beginnings, these were great achievements for me. More pleasing still, I never campaigned for any of the positions but

More and more entrepreneurs and businesspeople are looking to the second half of their lives to contribute to the social good. Some do it by running for office. Others do it by teaching school. Still others set up foundations that help fund causes important to the founder. What will you do with your second half?

was given or nominated for them by the public as a reflection of the good opinion they had of me. I held my position in the Assembly for ten years in a row in this manner.

PART III

The Legacy of an Entrepreneur

CHAPTER 59

The Power of Contingent Contracts

Franklin shares one of his most creative solutions with us in this chapter, showing us the power of sharing risk through contingent contracts. When two parties adamantly disagree about possible future events, don't let the disagreement escalate into a conflict. Rather, use the disagreement as the basis of a contingent contract, focusing both parties on the future by spreading the risk appropriately. Sometimes the solution is built upon the very nature of the conflict itself.

IN 1751, MY FRIEND DR. THOMAS BOND SHARED with me his idea of establishing a public hospital in Philadelphia. At the time, there were no hospitals in America and Dr. Bond experienced a great deal of difficulty in getting people to understand the basic idea. In consequence, his prospects for funding the project were very low despite his great enthusiasm. Ultimately, he came to my door seeking help, claiming that no public project could succeed in this area without my involvement. "I am often asked by those I approach," he told me, "if I have consulted you on this matter. When I tell them that I have not, they respond only that they will 'consider the matter' and I never hear back from them."

Taking the opportunity, we consulted with one another about his proposal. I was so impressed with what I heard that I immediately pledged funds and set about helping him raise money for the project. As was my common practice, I hoped to prepare the minds of the people before the fundraising began. I did this by writing about the project in my newspaper. Dr. Bond, in contrast, had done nothing to prepare the minds of his listeners, and this had contributed to his failure in raising funds.

We experienced great success in fundraising at this point, but I soon discerned that we would need to take even stronger measures if the idea were to become a reality. I brought the matter before the Assembly, and it was opposed by the members living outside the city. Those members from the country contended that the hospital would benefit only people who lived in the city, and that therefore the city's citizens alone should bear the expense of the project. Furthermore, they raised doubts as to whether the citizens of the city even approved of such an undertaking. I countered that I was certain of raising 2,000 pounds in voluntary donations, but they scoffed at my confidence.

Since Franklin's day, business and public health have gone hand in hand. John D. Rockefeller's foundation funded work that eradicated the hookworm in the southern United States. The Bill & Melinda Gates Foundation keeps a number of initiatives working to improve health worldwide.

With this kind of opposition, I decided to draft the bill with a contingency clause. Here's how it worked: If voluntary contributions for the hospital reached or exceeded 2,000 pounds and the project put in place a governing board, the Assembly would match these funds with another 2,000 pounds. If the voluntary contributions did not reach this amount, then the Assembly was under no obligation to provide matching funds. The 2,000 pounds from the Assembly would go toward funding the construction and operation of the hospital building. The annual interest from the 2,000 pounds in voluntary donations would be dedicated to providing funds so that the poor in the community could receive care and medication at no cost.

This contingency clause successfully won a majority of votes for the bill by spreading the risk among all involved. The clause helped the opposition in the Assembly realize that they could get credit for being charitable without running the risk of appearing foolish to their constituents. The clause not only won their votes but helped us gain support outside of the Assembly. In our fundraising efforts, we pointed to the conditional promise of the law as an additional reason to give to the project, since it effectively doubled the impact of everybody's donation. Needless to say, our fundraising soon topped 2,000 pounds, and we petitioned for and received the promised public gift. The hospital was soon built and continues to flourish to this day. Personally, I can't recall a time when a creative solution to a politically divisive situation gave me more pleasure than this particular situation. I still consider it one of my finest moments; conflict was avoided and everyone on the other side was happier and better off.

> POOR RICHARD ONCE SAID, "BE NEITHER SILLY, NOR CUNNING, BUT WISE."

CHAPTER 60

Good Advice for Fundraising

In this chapter Franklin demonstrates the power of social proof. That is, people often look to others for a social cue when they are uncertain about how to act. In the absence of authority, watch how Franklin uses the power of peers to legitimize an otherwise unknown project. Persuasion expert Dr. Robert Cialdini notes, "Influence is best exerted horizontally rather than vertically."

NOT LONG AFTER THE SUCCESS IN ESTABLISHING the hospital, the Reverend Gilbert Tennent approached me with another fundraising project. He wished to raise money for a new meeting house for a group of Presbyterians who had originally been followers of the Reverend George Whitefield. I absolutely refused to help on the principle that I did not wish to anger my fellow citizens by constantly asking them for money. Having failed in his first request, he then asked if I would simply furnish him the names of the generous people who always seemed to support the projects I championed. I refused this request also, being unwilling to create a beggar's market among my kind and generous friends.

He then asked if I would at least give him a bit of advice. "That I will readily do," I responded.

I advised him to ask first for money from those people whom he was certain would give to his cause. Next, approach those people about whom he was uncertain and show them the list of people who had already given. They might contribute once they knew who else supported the project. Finally, go ahead and ask those people he thought would never give to his project. More than once I've misplaced my certainty and secured a gift from someone I knew would reject me.

> **POOR RICHARD ONCE SAID, "GREAT-ALMS-GIVING, LESSENS NO MAN'S LIVING."**

The Reverend Tennent laughed heartily and thanked me for my counsel. He approached his task according to my advice and obtained a much larger sum than he ever expected. He used the money to erect the elegant and spacious meeting house that still stands on Arch Street.

CHAPTER 61

Negotiating Peace with the American Indians

From this point forward, Franklin's autobiography is, by and large, the story of a public citizen drawing upon his business knowledge to help solve public problems. Throughout the autobiography, Franklin has dealt harshly with people who love drinking to excess. Here he deals harshly with an entire society whose leadership promotes excessive drinking. Although taking them to task on the matter of drunkenness, Franklin also held great admiration for the American Indian cultures and modeled some of his first attempts at a colonial union on the Iroquois League of Six Nations.

IN 1753, THE CROWN DECREED THAT THE COLONIES should renegotiate their peace treaties with the American Indians. Governor Hamilton appointed one of his advisors for the task and asked the Assembly to nominate some of their members to join in the endeavor. The Assembly nominated me and the speaker of the house, Mr. Norris. The three of us then traveled to Carlisle to meet with the Natives.

These particular American Indians had a reputation for drunkenness and were violent and disorderly when in this condition. In consequence, everyone in the region was strictly forbidden to sell them any alcohol until our business with them was concluded. Having brought no alcohol of their own with them, they complained loudly about this restriction. We answered them that everyone was better off if they remained sober during the treaty negotiations. When the negotiation was completed, we promised to provide them all the rum they wished to drink. They agreed to these terms and—with the compliance of the local citizens and merchants—everyone remained sober throughout the negotiation.

The new treaty was negotiated in an orderly manner and concluded to everyone's mutual satisfaction. Before the day was out, the Indians requested and received the promised rum. Nearly one hundred Indian men, women, and children were living in a temporary camp just outside the city. Their party was a large one. In the evening, a great noise arose from the direction of their camp, and we went out to investigate. We discovered that they had made a great bonfire in the middle of their camp, and by its light we could tell that their drunkenness had resulted in general chaos. Men and women alike were running around the camp half-naked, fighting and beating one another with firebrands. Their quarreling by the great bonfire, accompanied as it was by a horrible screaming, brought to mind all of those stories about hell we had been told in church. As there would be no stopping the unrest, we thought it best to return to the safety of our lodgings. At midnight, a number of them banged on our door demanding more rum. We ignored their repeated requests; they gave up, and finally left us alone.

Knowing they had caused a great disturbance, three of their elders came to us the next day to apologize. The elder who spoke acknowledged the trouble and laid the blame squarely on the rum. He then gave this curious defense of the rum saying, "The Great Spirit, who created all, made everything on the earth for some use. And a thing should always be put to use in accordance with its created purposes. Now when He made rum He said, 'Let this be for the American Indians to get drunk with,' and so this is why we drink rum as we do." Whether or not God desires that they drink rum as they do,

> POOR RICHARD ONCE SAID, "BE AT WAR WITH YOUR VICES, AT PEACE WITH YOUR NEIGHBORS, AND LET EVERY NEW-YEAR FIND YOU A BETTER MAN."

their drinking of it to excess is certainly contributing to their quick demise. In fact, rum has already annihilated many of the tribes who formerly inhabited the Northeast coast.

CHAPTER 62

———❖———

It's the Little Things

Franklin convincingly demonstrates in this chapter that quality of life lies both in the big projects as well as in the small details. Unintended side effects often accompany big improvement programs, and these irritants must be removed, too. Franklin shows us that the thousands of dollars spent on paving the streets could have been lost were it not for a few dollars' worth of labor. At the time, approximately 15,000 people lived in Philadelphia in 2,000 to 3,000 houses.

PHILADELPHIA IS A WONDERFULLY DESIGNED CITY. Its streets are large and straight and form a perfect grid. Unfortunately, these streets for many years went unpaved. In rainy weather, carriage wheels turned the streets into a quagmire impossible to cross. Dry weather brought its own misery: the swirling dust made life along the streets quite irritating.

I lived near one of the market areas and watched despairingly as the customers waded in mud as they purchased their goods. At last, the market area was paved with brick, giving everyone who came there firm footing (though they might be up to their ankles in mud while getting there). With a bit of talking and writing on the subject, we managed to get much of the surrounding area paved with stone. This allowed easy, dry access to the market for the numerous families living in nearby houses. Other streets remained unpaved, however, and whenever a carriage came up out of the mud and onto the pavement, the stones quickly became covered with mud. Worse yet, nobody took responsibility for removing the mud.

Thus, I looked around and found a poor but hard-working man who was willing to undertake the job of keeping the pavement clear of mud. For a small salary paid by the surrounding residents each month, he agreed to sweep the area twice per week and carry off all the dirt. As was my habit, I wrote and printed a pamphlet describing the advantages gained by all—particularly the merchants—for such a small fee. The pamphlet was distributed throughout the neighborhood and the project was unanimously supported when I made the rounds a few days later. The money was collected and the plan proved a great success. People throughout the city were delighted by the cleanliness that now characterized the marketplace, and from this small experiment rose a call for paving the streets throughout the city. The citizens even voiced a willingness to be taxed for such a project.

Soon after, I introduced a bill in the Assembly for paving the city. It passed while I was traveling to England a few years later but was altered a bit from my original design. I disagreed with the method by which the Assembly decided to assess and collect the tax, but I was delighted to learn that the bill now also carried provisions for lighting the city. Some people credit me with the idea for lighting the city but the honor belongs to the late Mr. John Clifton. He was the first to demonstrate the usefulness of public lamps by placing one at his door and keeping it lit after dark. I merely followed his example to help people see the benefit of lighting a city.

I will take some credit, however, in changing the design of the lamps. Clifton and I purchased our first lamps from London. They were standard globe lamps and had several flaws in their basic design. Having no way to admit a flow of air from the bottom of the globe, the smoke from the flame did not readily exit the top of the lamp. Instead, it swirled around inside the lamp, gradually collecting as soot on the inside of the lamp. The soot not only dimmed the light of the lamp but also had to be cleaned daily, which risked breaking the globe entirely.

I redesigned the lamp to consist of four flat panes with a long funnel above them to draw up the smoke, and crevices beneath to admit air from below to help move the smoke up the funnel. This design moved the smoke up and out, thereby keeping the panes clean. As such, our lamps did not grow dark before midnight as the London lamps do but continued bright until morning. Furthermore, any accident while cleaning the lamp would break but one easily replaceable pane rather than the whole globe. The solution was so simple it's a wonder to me that the people of London put up with such poor lighting. Then again, Londoners love nothing more than to sleep all day, stay awake all night, and complain about the high price of candles.

> POOR RICHARD ONCE SAID, "WHAT IS SERVING GOD? 'TIS DOING GOOD TO MAN."

Some readers might think smoke and dust to be trivial matters not worth relating in one's life story. Certainly, dust blown into the eyes of a single person or a single shop on a windy day is but a minor irritant. Yet this happens frequently in a city as large as Philadelphia, and dust blown into the eyes of the entire population can shut down a city. So think carefully before you turn away from those who give attention to small matters such as these. Human happiness is not so much a result of lucky events that rarely come our way. Rather, happiness is more often a result of the little advantages that accumulate every day.

If you want to make the world a better place, do something as basic as teaching a poor young man how to shave himself and keep his razor in good shape. In doing this, you may contribute more to his happiness in life than by giving him a lump sum of money. Money easily gained is often foolishly spent and later regretted, but a good skill pays dividends for a lifetime. By learning to shave, he escapes a lifetime of waiting for barbers, along with the dull razors and numerous germs that can accompany the experience. Rather, he can shave whenever it's convenient for him and know the pleasure that comes only with well-kept equipment and careful attention. It is with such sentiments that I have shared the preceding stories, hoping they might inspire people to continue improving the cities in this nation that I love so dearly.

————◦∗◦————

CHAPTER 63

The Reluctant Revolutionary

Franklin created one of the first plans for the unification of the American colonies. Interestingly enough, this unification would have been under the protection of the Crown, possibly avoiding the Revolutionary War entirely. Franklin greatly preferred peaceful solutions to military conflict. With this in mind, he looks back over this time of his life and wonders what might have happened if the Crown had decided differently.

IN 1753, I RECEIVED A JOINT APPOINTMENT, ALONG with Mr. William Hunter, to the position of postmaster-general for all the British colonies in America. For several years prior I had worked as comptroller for my predecessor, so I had a working knowledge of the finances of the postal system. The American post office had never made a profit even though Britain expected us to send them 600 pounds each year. Making the postal system profitable required some expensive improvements, and we suffered a loss of 900 pounds for each of the first four years. The next year, however, our investment began to repay itself and the post office maintained a profit of about 3,000 pounds per year. Years later, I lost my position owing to events during the Revolution. After my untimely removal, the postal system again started losing money.

Shortly after my appointment to postmaster-general, I was grateful to receive two honorary college degrees during some business travel in New England. Both Yale, in Connecticut, and Harvard, near my hometown of Boston, presented me with the degree of Master of Arts. These were given to me in recognition of my scientific discoveries in the study of electricity, which I will describe in a later section.

In 1754, it looked as though war with France was once again imminent. The Board of Trade in Britain ordered each of the colonies to send commissioners to Albany where they would confer with the chiefs of the Six Nations—a confederacy of six Iroquois tribes. The goal of the meeting was to ensure that the Six Nations would fight on our side should war break out with the French. Governor Hamilton once again appointed me and Mr. Norris to serve as commissioners in these negotiations and we were joined this time by Mr. John Penn and Secretary Peters. Though the House did not approve of the negotiations being held outside of Pennsylvania, they approved our appointments and also the governor's request for gifts for the Indians. We traveled to Albany and met with the other commissioners about the middle of June.

As we traveled to Albany, I took the opportunity to draw up a plan for the unification of all the colonies under one government. Defending ourselves against aggressors was easier as a union, I contended, and there were other benefits as well. As we passed through New York, I shared my plan with two friends with a great knowledge of public affairs, Mr. James Alexander and Mr. Archibald Kennedy. These two learned

> **POOR RICHARD ONCE SAID, "NECESSITY NEVER MADE A GOOD BARGAIN."**

men agreed that the plan was solid, and I decided then to lay out the plan at the commissioner's meeting in Albany.

When the meetings began in Albany, I was pleased to learn that several other commissioners had formed similar unification plans. The matter of establishing a union was laid before the commissioners and it passed unanimously. A committee was then appointed with one commissioner from each colony to study the several plans that were known to be at the meeting. My plan was chosen by the committee and, with a few amendments, was recommended to the entire assembly.

My plan suggested that a unified government be established and administered by a president-general, who would be appointed and supported by the Crown. To provide some balance, the president-general's council of advisors would be chosen by the assemblies of the various colonies. The commissioners in Albany debated the plan daily, in addition to the business with the Six Nations. After a spirited debate, the plan was unanimously approved and copies of it were sent to the Board of Trade and to the assemblies of the various colonies. Governor Hamilton of Pennsylvania sent my plan to the Assembly with a strong recommendation of approval. An opponent of the plan, however, managed to have it debated when I was out of town, which I thought very unfair. Without me there to advocate for it, it was quickly rejected.

Unfortunately, the plan met with a swift death in every other locale, too. The colonial assemblies rejected it, believing that it gave the Crown too much power. In contrast, it was rejected in London for being perceived as too democratic. In its place, the Board of Trade formed another plan they claimed better served the same purposes. In this plan, the governors of each of the provinces, along with some members of their councils, could meet and order the raising of troops and building of forts for the common defense. The colonies could borrow the necessary money from the Crown's treasury, and it would be repaid later by Parliament levying a tax on the American colonies.

The Albany meetings lasted for months and I decided to spend the following winter in Boston. During my stay, I conversed often with Governor Shirley of Massachusetts regarding the advantages and disadvantages of both plans. I am still of the opinion that my plan was the better one and might have kept the peace between the Crown and the American colonies. Had the colonies been given the chance to unite on their own terms, they would have been sufficiently strong to provide for their own defense and pay for it themselves. The opposing plan ultimately required troops from England, and the cost of the troops was recouped by taxes imposed by the Parliament. This, in my opinion, set us on the road to the Revolution. Such mistakes are not new, however, and rulers throughout history have made similar ones. Rulers are often so overwhelmed with the pressures of government that they rarely take time to consider new ideas—even good ones. When it comes to power and politics, convenience often trumps intelligence.

CHAPTER 64

How to Get Off to a Bad Start

Harsh beginnings can start a vicious cycle from which there is often no recovery, and this is especially true when it comes to leadership. This chapter introduces a new governor of Pennsylvania and details how he made his administration unnecessarily difficult. Elsewhere Franklin wrote of Governor Morris, "He has 1000 little tricks to provoke and irritate the people, but none to gain their goodwill, esteem, or confidence." This chapter also describes an episode in which Franklin was probably offered a bribe to turn on the Quakers and side with the governing authorities. Whatever the governor's intent, Franklin was clearly uncomfortable with the atmosphere and the talk around the table. Despite the tone of the conversation at the table, readers should note that Franklin's last public act was for the abolition of slavery.

DURING MY TRAVELS IN NEW YORK THAT YEAR, I met our incoming governor, Mr. Robert Morris, whom I had met briefly in England. He had just arrived from there and would soon replace Governor Hamilton who, weary from the pressures of governing, had recently resigned. Mr. Morris asked me if he should also expect difficulty in governing the Quaker-controlled colony. "No," I replied to the contrary. "You can expect a very pleasant tenure as long as you take care not to cause unnecessary disputes with the Assembly."

"My dear Franklin," he responded, "why do you advise against my causing disputes? You know I love political disputes and believe them to be one of life's great pleasures. However, to demonstrate my regard for you, I promise to do my absolute best to avoid them." His love of political disputes was not unfounded. He was very eloquent and intelligent as a speaker, and he generally won any argument he either started or entered. Like me, he had been bred to his talents. I heard that his father trained his children for dispute by having them argue with him and one another while sitting at the dinner table. I counsel parents against this practice, however. During the course of my life, I have found people who love disputation and argument to be generally unsuccessful in their affairs. Of course, they sometimes achieve a victory but they never acquire goodwill, which would be of more use to them.

We parted ways, him going to Philadelphia and me to Boston. On my way home, I received news while in New York of the votes of the Assembly since his arrival. Despite his promise to me, he and the House had begun to battle with one another and, for that matter, it continued as long as he was governor. When I returned to my seat in the Assembly, I was soon given the job of writing our official responses to his speeches and messages. Our answers and his responses were often sharp and sometimes downright abusive. He knew I wrote for the Assembly, and one might think that he'd be ready to slit my throat should our paths cross. Despite his love of disputation, he was a good-natured man who never allowed personal differences to spoil a friendship. As a result, we often dined together.

POOR RICHARD ONCE SAID, "AVOID DISHONEST GAIN: NO PRICE CAN RECOMPENCE THE PANGS OF VICE."

One afternoon, when his battle with the Assembly was at its peak, we happened to meet one another in the street. He invited me to dinner, took me by my arm, and led me to his home. After a wonderful dinner, wine was served all around and the conversation turned quite merry. Apparently joking and somewhat ineptly, he announced to all that he thought Sancho Panza had been right all along. When asked to govern, Sancho Panza requested a government of blacks so if he could not agree with his subjects he could sell them instead.

One of the governor's friends then said to me, "Franklin, why do you continue to side with those annoying Quakers? Wouldn't you be better off if you sold them? The Penn family would give you a good price if you did." As a way out, I retorted that, "The governor has not yet succeeded in 'blackening' them." Indeed, he had worked hard to blacken the reputation of the Quakers in all his messages but they wiped off his smears as fast as he laid them on. In response, they flung them back thick upon his face in such quantity that, like his predecessor, he resigned as governor rather than suffer further damage to his reputation.

CHAPTER 65

Death and
Taxes

Franklin's business experience routinely made him an increasingly effective public servant. In this chapter, he engages in a wonderfully entrepreneurial financial move that allows people to lay claim to capital of which the government was unaware. When parties on both sides were crying that it must be either one way or another, Franklin shows us once again that third ways can be created. Remember to search hard for the third ways when stuck in dilemmas.

THE ROOT CAUSE OF EVERY ONE OF THESE PUBLIC quarrels was the proprietary system that originally governed the colonies. The Penn family fought viciously against those who wished to include their immense land holdings in any property tax law put forward to raise money for the common defense. They even went so far as to financially punish any governor or other appointed official who didn't support their wishes. The Assembly held out against this charade for three years but out of necessity passed a law exempting the Penn family's land from taxes. Thankfully, Governor Morris's successor, Captain Denny, overturned this law and I'll tell you how he did so shortly. In the meantime, let me share another episode about Governor Morris, though you already know the end of his story.

The French-Indian War had now begun and the Massachusetts Bay Colony expected an attack upon Crown Point on Lake Champlain. The government commissioned two men, Mr. Quincy and Mr. Pownall, to travel to Pennsylvania and ask for help. Knowing me to be from Boston and to also be an influential member of the Assembly, Mr. Quincy came directly to seek my counsel on the matter. I took it upon myself to present his request to the Assembly and it was well received. They voted to provide 10,000 pounds' worth of assistance to be given in provisions. Governor Morris refused to sign the bill, however, unless it included an amendment exempting the Penn family's vast land holdings from any tax levied for the purpose of defense. Thus, the Assembly and the governor were in a standoff with one another and things began to escalate. Mr. Quincy even lobbied the governor but he only dug further into his position.

As a way out, I proposed a way of raising the money that would not require the approval of the governor. By law, the Assembly could withdraw funds from the Loan Office as needed. At that time, there was little or no money in the Loan Office so I proposed that the Loan Office issue bonds redeemable in one year at a 5 percent interest rate. The Assembly adopted the proposal immediately, knowing the public would eagerly purchase enough bonds to fund the 10,000 pounds requested by Mr. Quincy.

The bonds were backed by the combined principal and interest of all loans outstanding from the Loan Office. Because this amount was far greater than the total of the bonds issued, the bonds obtained instant credit in the public market and sold quickly. Merchants considered them as good as cash for purchasing some of Quincy's provisions, and many wealthy citizens of the province who had cash to spare invested in these bonds due to their favorable interest rate and liquidity. We sold all 10,000 pounds' worth within a few weeks, and some were passed around in place of cash. Thus, we solved the problem without raising taxes or further escalating with the governor. Mr. Quincy publicly thanked the Assembly and returned to the Massachusetts Bay Colony a hero. He and I remained good friends from then on.

> POOR RICHARD ONCE SAID, "THE CREDITORS ARE A SUPERSTITIOUS SECT, GREAT OBSERVERS OF SET DAYS AND TIMES."

CHAPTER 66

How to Gain Cooperation

Once again in this chapter Franklin puts his business experience to use in motivating people to volunteer for public projects. Using the power of advertisements and contracts, Franklin gains the cooperation of an entire region when others would probably have failed. This chapter is a true masterpiece of persuasion. Note how Franklin vividly illustrates the consequences of noncooperation, and that he was also smart enough to set a deadline. On top of this, he makes a great first impression on an important new official.

AS YOU MAY RECALL, THE CROWN REJECTED OUR plan at Albany for uniting the colonies. I suspected that King George would never allow us to unify for our mutual defense, lest the colonies gain some sense of their own military strength. In place of this, they sent over General Braddock, along with two regiments of regular English troops, to help defend us against the French and Indians. Braddock landed at Alexandria in Virginia and marched north to Fredericktown in Maryland, where he hoped to supply himself for the coming wilderness campaign.

The Quakers in our Assembly had already heard that the general despised them for their pacifist views. I was sent to visit General Braddock in hopes of improving our image. To ease the tensions, I chose to visit in my capacity as postmaster-general rather than as a member of the Assembly. This way, I could begin talking about how to best handle his military dispatches and personal correspondence and then ease into other topics. My son, William, who now had some experience as a soldier in the King's service, went with me on this visit.

We found the general at Fredericktown in Maryland fuming about the slow return of the troops he had sent into the rural areas of Virginia and Maryland to procure wagons to carry supplies for his campaign. This delay allowed me to visit with him for several days. We dined together regularly, and I took the chance to soften his prejudices by sharing with him what the Assembly had already done and what they were standing ready to do to help him succeed in his campaign. I was about to depart when the long-expected supply wagons were brought to the camp. Braddock's soldiers had managed to get hold of only 25 wagons, and some of these were in a condition unsatisfactory for use in a wilderness campaign. The general and his officers exploded at this point and declared their campaign over before it had a chance to begin. Furthermore, they cursed the defense ministers in England for sending them into rural lands so poverty-stricken that they could never obtain the 150 wagons necessary to move their army.

> POOR RICHARD ONCE SAID, "IF YOU'D HAVE IT DONE, GO: IF NOT, SEND."

At this precise moment, I offered that I thought it a shame that the ministers had not sent them instead to Pennsylvania, where every farmer had his own wagon. General Braddock overheard my comment and said, "You seem to have a great deal of influence in Pennsylvania. Why don't you solve this problem for us?" I responded that to do so I needed to put the general's terms in writing for all to read, and we negotiated those terms immediately. You can read these terms for yourself in the advertisement I published as soon as I returned to Pennsylvania. It succeeded as well as anything I've done, and I've inserted the entire document next for you to examine.

ADVERTISEMENT
LANCASTER, April 26, 1755

His Majesty's defense forces will soon rendezvous at Will's Creek and are in need of 150 wagons drawn with four horses and 1,500 saddle or pack horses. Their leader, General Braddock, has given me authority to make contracts with any persons wishing to hire out their horses and wagons. I will be available for contracting in Lancaster County from today until next Wednesday evening and I will be in York County from next Thursday morning until Friday evening. His majesty's terms are as follows:

(1) Fifteen shillings per day will be paid for each wagon with four good horses and a driver. Two shillings per day will be paid for each able horse with its own pack-saddle or other saddle. Eighteen pence per day shall be paid for each able horse without a saddle.

(2) Payments begin when the equipment arrives at Will's Creek. All equipment must arrive on or before May 20. In addition, a reasonable allowance will be paid for the time necessary for traveling to and from Will's Creek.

(3) Each wagon, team, saddle, and pack horse will be valued by a neutral third party chosen jointly by me and the owner. Should any wagon, team, or horse be lost or destroyed while in the service of the military, the owner will be reimbursed the amount of this valuation.

(4) A seven-day cash advance will be paid by me to the owner of each wagon and team or horse at the time of contracting and the remainder of the amount will be paid by General Braddock (or his paymaster) at the time of their discharge or at some point prior should the time of service be prolonged.

(5) All drivers of wagons or persons taking care of hired horses are exempt from any and all kinds of military service during this contract. Their sole duty will be servicing their wagons and horses.

(6) A reasonable price will be paid for all oats, corn, or other horse food beyond what is necessary to feed the horses during their service. This food will be used by the army to feed their animals.

My son, William Franklin, is also empowered to enter such contracts with any person in Cumberland County.

"B. FRANKLIN."

TO ALL WHO LIVE IN LANCASTER, YORK, AND CUMBERLAND COUNTIES:

Friends and Fellow Citizens,

I have been at General Braddock's camp in Fredericktown, Maryland, the past few days. The general and his officers expected the citizens of Maryland to supply them with wagons and horses. Maryland has plenty of wagons and horses to spare but a conflict between the governor and the Assembly has prevented any money or attention from being put forth to solve this problem. As a result, the general and his men are quite frustrated.

Some among the general's council proposed sending soldiers immediately into Lancaster, York, and Cumberland Counties to seize as many good wagons and horses as necessary for military purposes. Furthermore, the army would force as many Pennsylvanians as necessary into service to drive these wagons and care for these horses.

Knowing them to be frustrated already, I suspected that the entry of British soldiers into these counties for the purpose of seizing property for military service would create a great deal of trouble for the citizens of these counties. I therefore thought it wise to attempt to negotiate fair and equitable terms for such service in lieu of outright seizure.

Being a member of the Assembly, I know that the people of these three rural counties have often complained that they are in constant need of currency. The general's need presents you with a marvelous opportunity of receiving and circulating among yourselves a great deal of currency. I expect these wagons and horses will be required for upwards of 120 days and this means that approximately 30,000 pounds will be paid to you in silver and gold of the king's money.

In comparison to farm work, the military service will be light and easy. At best, the army can only march 12 miles each day. The wagons and horses can never exceed this distance as they carry the army's basic supplies. Furthermore, the army has every incentive to keep these items safe and secure, whether on the march or in a camp.

If you are really the good and loyal subjects to His Majesty that I know you to be, you now have the chance to do the king a great service and save yourselves from the inconvenience of seizure. If you lack the resources to do it alone, band together with others, with one providing the wagon and several others the horses and driver. Divide the pay among yourselves proportionate to your contribution. Should you fail to serve your king and country voluntarily, especially when such good terms and reasonable pay are offered in advance, your loyalty will be strongly suspected. Quite frankly, the king's business will be done with or without your cooperation. Many brave soldiers have come a great distance to defend you and they will not stand idle while you withhold providing what might reasonably be expected of you. The army will need wagons and horses and will most likely seize them if you are unwilling to offer them. Should this happen, few if any of you will receive fair payment for your sacrifice and none of you will be pitied or well-regarded.

The only return I expect for my efforts in this matter is the satisfaction that comes from doing the right thing. Should this offer for acquiring wagons and horses fail to persuade you, General Braddock has asked me to notify him after two weeks. At that time, I suppose his quartermaster, the fearsome Sir John St. Clair, and a regiment of soldiers will enter the province to start seizing the items instead. And I will be very sorry to hear that this has happened, because I am very sincerely and truly your friend and well-wisher,

"B. FRANKLIN"

General Braddock had given me 800 pounds for the purpose of paying advances to those who agreed to these terms. The response was so overwhelmingly positive that I had used 200 pounds of my own money to finish the job. Before two weeks had passed, 150 wagons and 259 pack horses were on their way to the general's camp. The advertisement promised to reimburse the owners should their wagon or horse be either lost or damaged while in use. General Braddock's word was not good enough for the owners, who did not know him. Instead, they asked me to post a bond guaranteeing payment in case of loss, and I agreed to their request.

———⟨⟩———

CHAPTER 67

How to Get Off to a Great Start

First impressions are indeed lasting impressions and Franklin continues to impress the British military in this section. He reminds us once again that we should always be asking ourselves, "Whom can I help here?" The newly arrived British officers were virtually helpless in getting the provisions they needed for a military campaign thousands of miles from their homeland. And this was just the kind of help the peaceloving Quakers loved to provide: food rather than firearms. This chapter may look like a shopping list but it's really a recipe for increasing your influence.

I DINED ONE EVENING AT THE GENERAL'S CAMP with the officers of Colonel Dunbar's regiment. Colonel Dunbar shared with me his concern that his subordinates were not wealthy men, and that food and drink were costly in the region. As a result, his men were having difficulty affording all the provisions they needed to buy for their expected long march through the wilderness. I acknowledged his views but promised no help at the time. Nonetheless, I silently resolved to

> **POOR RICHARD ONCE SAID, "GIFTS BURST ROCKS."**

do something more for them and wrote a letter to the Assembly the next morning. I recommended the officers to the Assembly and asked that some of the public money might be allocated toward supplying these officers with the necessary provisions for the campaign.

Drawing on his own military experience, my son created a list of necessary provisions, which I included in my letter to the Assembly. They approved the request immediately and, with the help of my son, the officers' provisions arrived at the same time the wagons pulled into camp. The Assembly had sent 20 individual packages, each containing:

Six pounds of refined sugar
Six pounds of brown sugar
One pound of good green tea
One pound of good black tea
Six pounds of good ground coffee
Six pounds of chocolate
Fifty pounds of good white biscuit
Half a pound of pepper
One quart high-quality white wine vinegar
One Gloucester cheese from England
Twenty pounds of good butter, packed in a keg
Two dozen bottles of aged Madeira wine
Two gallons of rum
One jar of mustard
Two well-cured hams
Six dried cow tongues
Six pounds of rice
Six pounds of raisins

These gifts were packed well, placed on 20 individual horses, and presented to each of the 20 intended officers. The officers were both surprised and pleased to accept the gifts, and the colonels from both regiments wrote very gracious letters of thanks. So satisfied was General Braddock both with his wagons and horses and with these unexpected gifts for his officers that he immediately settled accounts with me and requested my help in sending additional provisions his way. I worked quickly to fulfill his order, spending a little over 1,000 pounds of my own money to do it. I sent him the bill for these goods immediately, and he quickly returned to me a flat 1,000 pounds and rolled the remainder to the next bill. I never received the remaining 17 pounds, however, and will explain why after a brief word of caution.

A basket of fruit or food remains one of the quintessential business gifts. Yet, even this gesture got its start as a business. Los Angeles entrepreneur George C. Page virtually invented the fruit basket industry after tasting his first California orange. He created packaging which allowed him to ship the Golden State's fruits to other parts of the country as gift baskets.

CHAPTER 68

Guarding Against Overconfidence

In this short chapter, Franklin reminds us to remain cautious about things we cannot control. He also foreshadows a coming disaster.

I RETURNED TO PHILADELPHIA AND WAS APPROACHED by my friend Dr. Thomas Bond, with whom I had helped establish the hospital, with a curious proposition. As was now his practice, he and his brother came to me with a fundraising scheme for a grand firework show to celebrate what was sure to be Braddock's success in taking Fort Duquesne. With a grave look, I informed them that there would be time enough to prepare a celebration once we knew we had a reason for celebrating. Shocked that I didn't embrace their proposal they exclaimed, "Surely you don't believe Braddock will fail to take the fort!" I told them that I didn't know if the fort would or would not be taken. I did know, however, that matters of war are subject to great uncertainty. After hearing

> POOR RICHARD ONCE SAID, "'TIS EASY TO SEE, HARD TO FORESEE."

my counsel, they dropped the idea and were saved from the embarrassment they would have experienced had they prepared the firework show in advance. Dr. Bond later told me that he came to dislike "Franklin's forebodings."

———◆———

CHAPTER 69

Sizing Up the
British

*This chapter contains an account of Franklin's first experience with the
British army in combat. Braddock wasn't necessarily a fair view, however,
as he was far from the most talented general in the King's service.
Nonetheless, Franklin's conclusions are clear. While reading, keep in
mind that Franklin wrote this part of the autobiography many years after
the conclusion to the Revolutionary War. This helps explain why he's
happy to show kindness to his French friends while showcasing a tragic
loss to the British army. For the modern reader, these events are a good
reminder to never assume the market leader in any business situation is
invulnerable.*

GENERAL BRADDOCK WAS A BRAVE MAN AND WOULD have succeeded better
in some European war than he did in America. Unfortunately, he had too
much self-confidence, too high an opinion of his British troops, and held
too low an opinion of both Americans and the American Indians. One hundred local
troops joined him on his march, including our American Indian interpreter, George

Croghan. Such locals are always excellent guides, scouts, and such; but Braddock neglected them and they gradually left him. Before he left, he boasted somewhat about his intended progress. He said, "After taking Fort Duquesne, I will proceed immediately to Niagara and take it, too. Next, I expect to go on to Frontenac if the weather doesn't slow us down. I don't think it will, however, as Duquesne should fall in three or four days and then nothing should slow my march to Niagara."

I did not share his optimism. I knew that his army would have to cut its own road through the woods and bushes and that this would both spread them out and slow them down. Furthermore, I knew also that 1,500 French troops had marched into the Iroquois country only to go down in defeat. So I carefully measured my response, saying, "Indeed, Fort Duquesne is not yet fortified and we've heard that it holds only a small number of troops. If your excellent army arrives there healthy, it should most certainly be a quick battle. If I were going, the only danger I would watch out for is being ambushed by American Indians. They are masters of this tactic and your army could be an easy target, given its path. I suspect you'll be strung out for upwards of four miles. If ambushed, your army could be cut like a thread into several pieces, each unable to come to the other's defense."

With a smirk, Braddock disregarded my counsel saying, "These American Indians may be a formidable foe to your untrained colonial militias, but they do not stand a chance against the king's trained and disciplined troops." I knew better than to continue an argument with a general on the matter of his army. I said no more. I was wrong about one thing, however. The American Indians did not ambush his army when it was strung out for miles during the march. Rather, they let Braddock continue to build his confidence until he was within nine miles of Fort Duquesne.

His army had just crossed a river and were all bunched together as they marched through a rather open part of the forest. The first sign he had of trouble was a blistering attack on his advance guard. The Indians rained bullets upon them while hiding in the trees and bushes. The advance guard was thrown into confusion and the general rushed his remaining troops to join the fray. The new troops had to come through the wagon train, however, and this caused a great deal of confusion. As the troops rushed to the front of the line, the bullets

> **POOR RICHARD ONCE SAID, "HASTE MAKES WASTE."**

began coming from the sides instead. The officers on horseback were easy targets and they fell first. The soldiers, unorganized and having no one to give them orders, came under heavy fire and returned little. Soon, two-thirds of them were dead and the remainder fled in panic.

The civilian wagon drivers each took a horse from their team and fled, leaving all the wagons, provisions, and artillery to the enemy. General Braddock was mortally wounded and many soldiers perished bringing him off the field of battle. His secretary, Mr. Shirley, was killed at his side, and 63 of his 86 officers were killed or wounded. Of his 1,100 hand-picked soldiers, 714 were killed. Fortunately, half the army had been left behind with Colonel Dunbar, who was to follow Braddock with the heavier stores, provisions, and supplies once the main path had been cleared. The enemy chose not to pursue those who fled the ambush and these soon arrived at Dunbar's camp, causing a great deal of panic among the troops. Dunbar had well above 1,000 men and the enemy most likely didn't exceed 400 American Indians and French combined, given the reports. Rather than push forward and recover some of the lost honor, the panic-stricken Dunbar chose instead to run for cover to the nearest settlement.

> The history of capitalism is littered with the names of now defunct front-runners who were considered unbeatable in their day. Consider the fates of Woolworth's, Pan Am, Digital Equipment Corporation, Oldsmobile, and Studebaker whenever you think that your competitor is invulnerable.

So as to travel light and swift, he ordered all unnecessary supplies and ammunition destroyed—a mighty surplus given the recent losses. This did free up a number of horses and greatly reduced the number of supply wagons. When he got out of the wilderness, he was met with requests from the governors of Virginia, Maryland, and Pennsylvania that he turn back and post his troops along the frontier, where they gave some protection to the locals. He ignored these messages, however, and continued his hasty march all the way to Philadelphia, where he felt safe within the confines of the city. This entire incident signaled to us Americans that maybe we had overestimated the British, and suggested that our belief in their invulnerability was unfounded.

In fact, Braddock and his army gave offense from the moment they landed on our shores. On their first march from Alexandria to Fredericktown, they had plundered and stripped the locals of their supplies, completely ruining some poor families. Anyone who stood against the pillaging was, at best, insulted and, at worst, battered and confined to prison. We hadn't wanted their help in the first place, and this behavior only proved the idea was contemptible. Not every allied army behaved this way on our shores. When the French came over in 1781 to help us during the Revolution, their behavior was quite commendable. They marched from Rhode Island all the way to Virginia, nearly 700 miles, without complaint from the locals along the way. They never took a pig, chicken, or even an apple without paying the owner.

CHAPTER 70

Calling in Debts, Old and New

You will recall that Franklin posted a bond against the loss of the wagons and supplies that General Braddock used in his campaign. In other words, he put his reputation—and fortune—on the line to gain the cooperation of the locals. Here Franklin shows clearly that it's one thing to buy the insurance and it's another to get the money. With everything lost, the locals demanded payment from Franklin and he managed to get it. His effectiveness, however, was due to the preexisting personal relationship described in Chapter 63. Some might criticize Franklin for networking too much. However, his visiting local officials during his last trip to Boston saved him from financial ruin in this chapter.

I LEARNED OF GENERAL BRADDOCK'S FATE FROM one of his surviving officers, Captain Orme. Orme and the general were seriously wounded and brought off the field together. Braddock would die a few days later, with Orme recovering from injuries received at his side. Orme reported that the general was completely silent the entire first day and spoke only once when night fell saying, "Who would have thought it?" He was as silent the next day, saying only, "We shall better know how to deal with them the next time." These were his last words and he died a few minutes later.

The secretary's papers fell into the enemy's hands and these included not only the general's orders but numerous instructions and personal letters. They published a number of the papers and letters in French papers in order to prove the hostile intentions of the British crown prior to the formal declaration of war. Among those papers published were several letters, from Braddock to the Ministers in London, which spoke highly of the service I had rendered to the army. These were not the only letters he wrote, however. David Hume, who served in the ministry during this same period, informed me later that Braddock had sent several letters prior to these recommending my services. As the expedition was a complete failure, however, these letters of recommendation never did me any good.

> POOR RICHARD ONCE SAID, "MANY WOULD LIVE BY THEIR WITS, BUT BREAK FOR A WANT OF STOCK."

General Braddock had once asked me what favor he could return for my services to him. I asked only one: That he order his officers to stop enlisting our indentured servants and discharge those that had already been enlisted. Braddock granted the request immediately and, upon my identification, several indentured servants were soon returned to their masters. Colonel Dunbar proved less generous when he heard of the general's command. I came to him while he was housed in Philadelphia on his retreat—or, more accurately, flight. I requested the discharge of several indentured servants that he had enlisted from three poor farmers near Lancaster, reminding him of his late general's orders. He promised me that if the masters of these men would meet him in Trenton in a few days, he would return their servants to them as he marched to New York. I sent word to these farmers and they went to great trouble and expense to meet him there. Dunbar refused to deliver on his promise, however, to both their disappointment and personal loss.

The news of the loss of most of the wagons and horses spread quickly and all the owners came to me with their valuations to claim the money I was bonded to pay. They demanded that I deliver on my promise quickly, and I had few immediate answers for them. I could say only that I had written Braddock's successor, General Shirley, former governor of Massachusetts Bay Colony and a good friend. He was a great distance away, I explained, and could not answer quickly, but I assured them that their money was waiting in the paymaster's hands for these orders to arrive. I urged them to have patience. Some refused and began to sue me for the money. I managed to keep their cases at bay until we got a response from the general. Thankfully, he appointed commissioners to examine the claims and order payment when satisfied. The claims totaled nearly 20,000 pounds. Paying the claims would have brought me to financial ruin had General Shirley not stood by the promise of his predecessor.

CHAPTER 71

Negotiating with Coalitions

The politics associated with the funding of the defense project between the pacifist Quakers and the tax-averse Penn family kept Franklin very busy. In this episode he shows us yet another way of breaking a negotiation stalemate. In the midst of a deadlock, another party enters the conflict and shifts the balance of power. Next time you are in a difficult negotiation, ask yourself, "Who else could join us at the table?" A third party added to either side of the table sometimes provides the necessary change in dynamics.

AS YOU MAY RECALL, BEFORE BRADDOCK'S DEFEAT, Governor Morris had continually harassed the Assembly about their attempts to pass a bill that taxed the Penn family's estates in providing for the common defense. Hearing the news of Braddock's defeat, he doubled his attacks, hoping to capitalize on what seemed to be a near and present danger to speed his version of the bill through with tax exemptions for the Penn family intact. The Assembly, however, did not waver. Justice, they thought, was on their side and rubber-stamping the governor's wishes was an abdication of their responsibilities.

> **POOR RICHARD ONCE SAID, "CUNNING PROCEEDS FROM WANT OF CAPACITY."**

Toward the end of the struggle, the Assembly had passed a bill for raising 50,000 pounds in property taxes for defense. Governor Morris was willing to sign it if he could change only one word. Was the impasse at an end? The bill read, "that all estates, real and personal, were to be taxed, those of the Penn family not excepted." He wished to change the wording from "not excepted" to "only excepted." One word, for sure, but a mighty important one! When news of his maneuverings reached England, some of our friends there came to our aid.

We had been careful to furnish them with copies of the Assembly's responses to the governor's attacks. Our friends raised a public uproar against the Penn family for their heartlessness in giving their governor such orders. Some even went so far as to state that by refusing to help defend the province they forfeit their right to it. This last statement intimidated them to the point that they sent over 5,000 pounds of their own money as a free gift to the Assembly to use for any purpose we chose.

The Assembly accepted the gift in lieu of a tax on their estates and a new bill was passed with a clause officially exempting them. As I had helped champion this bill, it appointed me as one of the commissioners charged with spending the defense fund, which ended up being 60,000 pounds. At the same time, I had passed through the Assembly another bill for establishing and training a voluntary militia (taking great care, of course, to not offend the Quakers). This was a welcome victory, given the trouble that accompanied our previous efforts at passing a militia law.

———⟫◉⟪———

CHAPTER 72

Benjamin Franklin, Soldier

Franklin had been engaged in the defense of the colonies for some time now. He'd worked closely with the British army, procured cannons, and even stood watch with the militia. At this point, he becomes a soldier with a full military commission from the governor. Over the next few chapters, watch how Franklin deftly applies his business savvy to his military command. The result is a surprisingly effective officer.

THE TASK NOW WAS TO GET VOLUNTEERS FOR the emerging military conflict, and I helped do this by publishing a pamphlet promoting the militia. Hundreds of people stepped forward and formed companies throughout the city and countryside to begin training. Governor Morris asked me to take charge of the northwestern frontier which was already overrun by the enemy. I undertook the business of raising troops and building forts even though I didn't perceive myself as particularly qualified for this. The governor commissioned me with full military powers and gave me a number of blank commissions to bestow upon anyone I chose to be an officer. There was no difficulty raising troops and soon I had 560 men under my command. My son William, having served as an army officer in the war against Canada, served very effectively as my chief assistant.

We set out upon the business of building forts in January of 1756. I ordered one set of troops to the upper Minisink country with instructions to secure that country by erecting a fort, and another set did the same for the lower Minisink country. I traveled with the remainder of the troops to the Moravian settlement of Gnadenhut on the northwestern frontier, where a fort was immediately necessary. The American Indians had recently burned the village there and killed most of the inhabitants, so it was a good place for a show of strength. We marched there from Bethlehem, the chief Moravian settlement, supplied with five wagons by the locals.

> POOR RICHARD ONCE SAID, "HE THAT CAN-NOT OBEY, CANNOT COMMAND."

Bethlehem was already in a defensive posture, the Gnadenhut massacre having raised the specter of danger among the inhabitants. We found the main buildings in town protected by a stockade housing a good quantity of arms and ammunition purchased from New York. Furthermore, every high window in the town had beside it a stock of paving stones that could be thrown down upon the heads of any enemy attempting to enter the house. An armed watch had been organized in the city and functioned as efficiently as any professional military. All of this surprised me because, like the Quakers, the Moravians had obtained an act from the Parliament exempting them from military duties in the colonies. I asked their Bishop Spangenberg about the reality of their pacifist principles. He responded that pacifism was not currently one of their established principles. At the time the act was passed, he said, he recalled it being a principle of many Moravians. When they took a poll after the massacre at Gnadenhut, they found that few among the present population believed in the principle. I suppose they had either deceived themselves or deceived the Parliament. Nonetheless, common sense when pressed by current danger, will often prove too strong for whimsical opinions.

Just before we left Bethlehem, 11 farmers who had been driven from their farms by the Indians came to me requesting guns that they might go back and retrieve their livestock. I supplied each of them with a gun and plenty of ammunition. They set out immediately and we followed later that day. It started to rain shortly after our march began and it continued through the day. The wilderness offered us no shelter and we were as wet as water could make us. Toward night-fall, we came upon the house of a German fellow and huddled together in his barn for shelter. Had we been attacked that rainy day, we most certainly would have suffered great loss as we could not keep our guns and powder dry. The Indians, in contrast, know many ways to keep guns and powder dry. We learned later that the Indians had attacked and killed 10 of the 11 farmers who had set out before us. The one who escaped told us that they could not fire their guns because the powder was wet with rain.

The rain stopped by morning, and we continued our march to the desolated Gnadenhut. We found there an abandoned saw mill with a good supply of cut boards that we used to build temporary shelters for ourselves. Having no tents and being once already soaked by rain, we were pleased with the find. Our first work after building these shelters was to properly bury the dead who had been quickly placed in shallow graves following the massacre.

———⊷⊶———

CHAPTER 73

Managing Morale

In this chapter, Franklin and his troops get to work securing their outpost. Ever the scientist, Franklin notes differences in morale on sunny days and rainy days and attributes the difference to something other than the weather. Like the example Franklin gives here, many of our modern management practices evolved from the realities of managing a ship on the high seas. Though much has changed since then, much has remained the same. Franklin's observations about productivity and morale still hold true today.

THE NEXT MORNING WE MARKED OUT OUR FORT. The circumference measured 455 feet and would require as many trees one foot in diameter. Our 70 axes were put to the task and our men made great use of them. The trees began falling so fast that I began to time the work with my watch. Two men could cut down a 14-inch-diameter pine in six minutes. Each pine made three posts of 18 feet in length with a point on one end.

While some men worked on felling trees, others dug a three-foot-deep trench along the diameter of the fort in which the posts would be planted. Our five wagons had been split in half by removing a pin which held the fore and hind parts of the wagons together. This gave us ten carriages with two horses each to haul the posts from the woods to where the fort was being constructed. As the posts went up, our carpenters built a platform all around about six feet off the ground upon which the men could stand to fire their guns through the holes. We had one small canon with us which we mounted on one of the corners of the fort. We fired it off as soon as it was fixed to let any enemy within hearing know that we had such a piece in our possession. Thus, we finished building our fort within a week though it rained so hard every other day that the men could not work.

During this time, I learned that people are best contented when they are most productive. For on sunny days when we worked, the men were peaceful and happy. Basking in a good day's work, the men spent their evenings in merry company. On rainy days, however, the men were irritable and defiant. In lieu of productivity, they spent their energy finding fault with their pork and bread at dinner. All of this reminded me of a sea captain who made it a rule to keep the men on his boat constantly at some kind of work. When his first mate once told him that they had done everything possible and there was no work left he replied, "Oh? Make them scour the anchor."

> POOR RICHARD ONCE SAID, "YOU MAY GIVE A MAN AN OFFICE, BUT YOU CANNOT GIVE HIM DISCRETION."

Our fort, however small, was a sufficient defense against the American Indians, who have no cannon. Having now secured our outpost and having a place to which we could retreat, we sent scouting parties to survey the countryside. We never found any of them but we did find the places in the nearby hills where they perched to watch our activities. The skill they employed in hiding their presence is worth mentioning. It being winter, a fire was a necessity, but a fire on the surface of the ground would by its light and smoke have indicated their presence to us.

To avoid detection, they had dug holes in the ground about three feet in diameter and about four feet deep. With their hatchets they would cut charcoal from the sides of burnt logs lying in the woods. Using these coals they made small, virtually smoke-free fires at the bottom of the holes and then would drop their

A surprising number of our modern management practices evolved from shipboard activities because sailing was one of the first organized business ventures. Business lingo like "he knows the ropes," "taking the wind out of his sails," "showing his true colors," and, of course, "down the hatch" all originated on the high seas.

legs down into them to keep their feet and legs warm. When done this way, neither light, nor flame, nor spark, nor smoke would give away their presence. Judging from how many of these holes we discovered, their number was not great. Better still, they must have decided that we were too numerous to attack with any hope of success.

———⊱◈⊰———

CHAPTER 74

Reward or Punish?

Nowhere is Franklin's application of business principles in a military setting better illustrated than in this story of his suggesting reward as a way of gaining the cooperation of the troops, rather than the more traditional military solution of inflicting punishment. Decades of social-science research conducted two centuries later support Franklin's observation about the comparative power of reward over punishment in changing behavior.

OUR COMPANY CHAPLAIN WAS A RATHER ENTHUSIASTIC Presbyterian minister named Mr. Beatty. He often complained to me that my fellow soldiers were almost always absent from his prayer meetings and sermons. As I reflected on his complaints, I recalled that each soldier was promised—in addition to pay and provisions—a quarter pint of rum every day. This rum was distributed twice daily, and I noted that the men in the company were always present to receive their portion.

> **POOR RICHARD ONCE SAID, "HOPE OF GAIN LESSENS PAIN."**

Recognition can be a company's least expensive reward. Create ways to recognize great accomplishments. When salespeople at one of Dell's call centers make a great sale, they can ring a bell hanging on the wall and people gather round and give them "high fives."

Having now conceived a plan, I responded to Mr. Beatty's complaint stating, "It might be below the dignity of a minister to serve as supplymaster of the company's rum. However, if you attain this position and serve out the rum immediately following your prayer meetings, I suspect the men would flock to you."

Mr. Beatty was granted the position and performed admirably with the aid of a few extra men who helped measure out the rum. As a result, almost every man in the company began attending his prayer services, some even arriving early. Although military law allows for severe punishment of any soldier consistently absent from the company's religious services, I believe that my plan for rewarding the attendance of these same services far more effective in gaining the willing cooperation of the soldiers.

CHAPTER 75

A Hero's Return

Franklin's star is clearly rising by this chapter—and it is rising to notice-ably high levels. Not only is he a well-respected citizen, but now he has performed admirably as a military leader in organizing troops for defense. Sensing a celebration, the publicity-shunning Franklin returns to Philadelphia earlier than expected, and at night, so as to miss a wel-coming parade he knew was being organized. Despite this effort, he can't keep his followers from giving him full military recognition. Before telling us this story, however, Franklin shares some of his observations about one of the many religious communities that inhabited the American colonies.

WE HAD JUST FINISHED BUILDING OUR FORT AND got it well stocked with supplies when I received a letter from Governor Morris. He had unex-pectedly called the Assembly to session and wished me to return if my business on the frontier no longer required my presence and attention. I also received letters from some of my friends in the Assembly urging my return. My goal of building three forts had been completed and the inhabitants on the frontier were now content to remain on their farms with such protection nearby. I decided to return to Philadelphia, especially since an experienced officer from New England, Colonel William Clapham, happened to visit our area and agreed to accept the command in my absence.

I gave him a commission and paraded the troops before him. I read them the commission and introduced him as their new commanding officer. Given his experience in fighting our enemy, he was much more fit than I to command them. After turning over command, I gave them some brief words of encouragement and took my leave. The troops escorted me as far as Bethlehem, where I rested for a few days to recover from the fatigue of command. The first night there I could hardly sleep, the bed in which I lay was such a contrast from sleeping on the floor of our fort wrapped only in a blanket or two.

> POOR RICHARD ONCE SAID, "A GOOD EXAMPLE IS THE BEST SERMON."

While in Bethlehem, I took some time to learn more about the life of the Moravians. Some of them had joined us at the fort and all those I had met were very kind. I discovered that they worked for the common good, ate at a common table, and slept in common dormitories. These dormitories were crowded, but I noticed they had drilled holes all along the wall just under the ceiling line to improve air circulation. The music at their church was marvelous as the organ was accompanied by violins, oboes, flutes, clarinets, and other wind instruments.

Unlike the practice of churches in Philadelphia, their sermons were preached to strictly segregated audiences. Sometimes it was the married men who gathered. At other times it was only their wives. This pattern continued along with young men, young women, and then small children. The sermon I observed was the one for the small children. They came in and sat on benches in rows. The boys were guided by a young man, their tutor, and the girls were guided by a young woman. The sermon was well-adapted for the mind of a child and delivered to them in a very pleasant manner. It made no demands upon them except that of being good. The children behaved very well but I thought them to be a bit too pale. I suspect that they were kept indoors too much and not allowed exercise sufficient for good health.

I had heard stories that Moravians arranged their marriages by casting lots, so I thought it smart to inquire about the matter while among them. My host told me that lots were used only under a particular set of circumstances. When a young man wished to marry, he informed his elders of his desire to do so. His elders then consulted the elder ladies who oversaw the young women. The elders of both sexes were well acquainted with the traits and personalities of those under their care and were in the best position to choose the most suitable match. Their elders' judgments were usually in harmony with one another. However, every now and then two or three young women were judged to be equally suitable for a young man. When this happened, a lot was cast to decide the match. I objected that unhappiness can often result when matches are made without the mutual consent of the parties. "Unhappiness can also happen," responded my host, "when you let the parties choose for themselves." I could not deny the truth of this response.

When I returned to Philadelphia, I discovered that the volunteer militia had continued strong in my absence. Almost all inhabitants who were not Quaker had stepped forward, formed themselves into companies, and chose their leadership in accordance with the new law. Dr. Bond had championed the cause in my absence and came to give me a detailed report of his activities. I suspected that my pamphlet had increased the number of volunteers more than any single act. Never knowing one's impact for certain, however, I remained quiet and let him tell me how much he had done to further the cause. I find it wise to let others enjoy their opinions when there is no sense in disputing.

The officers met and elected me colonel of the entire regiment. This time I accepted my role as commander-in-chief and felt great pride as 1,200 well-dressed men paraded in front of me for review. The regiment had a disciplined artillery company with six brass canons, which they could fire off 12 times every minute. This first regimental review occurred in front of my house. As the artillery passed, they saluted me by firing some rounds as they passed my front door. The noise rattled the house and several glasses in my electrical apparatus broke as they fell off the shelf. My time as colonel proved even more fragile for the reason that all of our commissions were overthrown when Parliament repealed our militia law in England not long after this.

———>◦∢⊂———

CHAPTER 76

Enemies Accumulate

Franklin's exit from Philadelphia is an interesting contrast to his entry to the city almost 33 years earlier (see Chapter 12). This show of military honor, in tandem with the parade from the last chapter, gives Franklin's political enemies a chance to strike some blows at his reputation. When offered the chance to become a general in this chapter, he detects political motives and wisely turns down the commission. His foes may have tried to use the promotion as evidence of Franklin's trying to seize military power along with his popularity—not an uncommon occurrence throughout history. Once again, his attempts to practice the virtue of humility saved him from a potential trap. An interesting historical footnote: Franklin first met George Washington on the trip to Virginia he mentions in this chapter.

I WAS ONLY A COLONEL FOR A SHORT TIME BUT LONG enough to cause trouble. As I set out on a trip to Virginia, the officers of my regiment came up with the idea that they should properly escort me all the way out of town. I knew nothing of their plans or I would have ordered them to abandon the idea. I've never thought it good policy to show off one's importance to others. Nonetheless, they came to my door just as I mounted my horse—30 or 40 in number and all dressed in their uniforms. Their little surprise greatly annoyed me, but I could not at that time avoid their escort. To make matters worse, as soon as we began to move, they drew their swords and rode with them held aloft the entire way through town.

Somebody sent word to the Penn family about this silly affair and they were infuriated. No such honor had been given Thomas Penn when he visited the province nor to any of his governors. Not that he would want this, mind you. He claimed it was only proper to provide such an escort for royalty. I don't know whether this is true or not. I was, and still am, ignorant about etiquette in such circumstances. This farce, however, only increased his already great hostility against me that began with my opposing in the Assembly the exemption of his estate from taxation.

I was very public in my opposition to this demand and did not oppose it without a great deal of conviction about the basic injustice of his request. Among the ministers in England, he accused me of being a threat to the King's sovereignty by preventing proper laws for the raising of money to pass the House. And now, he pointed to this parade with my officers as further proof of my wanting to overthrow the King's rule by force. He also tried to strip my office of postmaster-general for the colonies from me by appealing directly to the Postmaster General, Sir Everard Fawkener. His efforts, however, garnered me nothing other than the most gentle of reprimands.

> POOR RICHARD ONCE SAID, "WHO HAS DECEIV'D THEE SO OFT AS THY SELF?"

You would think that Governor Morris would have been more infuriated with me than the Penns. After all, he and I had continually sparred with one another on this militia bill. Nevertheless, he and I still enjoyed a most civil relationship with nary an interpersonal difference between us. I attribute his ability to maintain a good relationship with me, despite our vicious public dispute, to his being trained as a lawyer. Professionally speaking, he might view the two of us as advocates contending for our clients in a lawsuit—he for the Penns and me for the Assembly. This might help explain why he would sometimes come for a friendly visit to give me advice on a difficult point and, more rarely, take my advice in return.

He and I worked as one to supply Braddock's army. When the shocking news of Braddock's defeat arrived, I was among the first sent for by the governor as he sought counsel on how to prevent the flight of inhabitants from the rural counties. I can't remember my specific advice on this occasion, but I think I suggested to him that Colonel Dunbar should be ordered temporarily to post his troops on the frontiers to protect the inhabitants and then continue his military expedition once reinforcements arrived from the colonial militias.

Now that I had returned from the frontier a hero, Governor Morris requested that I continue Braddock's military expedition with the colonial militia in the face of Colonel Dunbar's apparent unwillingness to do so. He wished to make me a general and order me to go and take Fort Duquesne. I did not share in his high opinion of my military prowess, and I suspected that political motives drove his willingness to promote me to general. My current popularity would certainly facilitate the raising of men, and my influence in the Assembly would ensure the money to pay them. And all of this might be done without the taxing of the Penns' estate holdings. Surprised at my lack of interest in becoming a general, he dropped the idea.

Not long after, Governor Morris resigned his post and was replaced by Captain Denny. I'll close the book by sharing the part I played in public affairs under his administration. Before I do so, however, it might be a good idea to give some information about the rise and development of my scientific reputation.

CHAPTER 77

My Life as a Scientist

Franklin goes back in time in this chapter to tell us about his scientific endeavors and the resulting fame, but concludes right in the middle of the current story. From Thomas Edison to biotechnology, science and business have often gone hand in hand in America, and Franklin was there at the very beginning. Somewhat of an outsider, he also shows us that there's more than one way to stake an intellectual claim. Incidentally, other recipients of the Copley Medal include Charles Darwin, Albert Einstein, and James Watson and Francis Crick, co-crackers of the DNA code.

IN 1746, I HAPPENED TO MEET A DR. SPENCE IN Boston. He had just arrived there from Scotland and showed me some of his electrical experiments. He was not an expert in the matter and his experiments were conducted rather shoddily. Nonetheless, it was a new subject for me, and I was amazed and pleased with what I saw. Shortly after I returned to Philadelphia, our library company received a gift from Mr. Peter Collinson, a fellow in the Royal Society, which is the national academy of science among the British. He presented us with a glass tube alongwith some instructions for conducting electrical experiments. I thought it a perfect opportunity to replicate the experiments I had seen in Boston. After much practice, I performed them flawlessly and even learned some new ones after reading an account of electrical experiments from England. These electrical phenomena were so curious that my house was constantly full of people who came to witness the feats.

In order to share the wonder (and inconvenience) among my friends, I ordered a number of tubes blown at our local glass house. These new tubes allowed us to increase our number to several performers, and none of these succeeded like my neighbor, Mr. Ebenezer Kinnersly. He was an intelligent fellow but out of work at the time. I encouraged him to charge a small fee for attending his demonstrations and I helped him put together two lectures to accompany those demonstrations. The end result was a surprisingly effective educational product. To improve even more, he purchased professional instruments far better than the ones I had roughed out for myself. His lectures drew large crowds, and word of mouth increased both his popularity and his pocketbook. Ultimately, he took his show on the road and demonstrated his equipment throughout the colonies. He even traveled as far as the West Indies but had great difficulty conducting his experiments given the general humidity of the islands.

POOR RICHARD ONCE SAID, "HALF THE TRUTH IS OFTEN A GREAT LIE."

Grateful to Mr. Collinson for having presented us with the equipment that launched our endeavor, I decided to inform him of our progress. I wrote him several letters giving detailed accounts of our electrical experiments. He requested that these letters be read at a meeting of the Royal Society, but their initial impact was so small as to not even be recorded in their newsletter, *Transactions*. I wrote a paper for Mr. Kinnersley, detailing my thoughts regarding how lightning and electricity are one and the same thing. I sent this paper to my friend Dr. Mitchel, also a member of the Royal Society, who informed me that the paper had been read and was laughed at by the experts in the Society.

All this information, however, eventually found its way into the hands of one of the Court physicians, Dr. Fothergill. He thought the papers too important to be snubbed in private and advised Collinson to print them to see if they would be better received by the public. Collinson took them to Edward Cave, publisher of the highly influential *Gentlemen's Magazine*. Cave decided to print the papers as a pamphlet instead and asked Dr. Fothergill to provide a preface for the volume. Cave's judgment proved profitable. I continued sending letters and papers about my electrical experiments, and his initial pamphlet soon swelled to a handsome bound volume. Over time, he published five editions of the work, sold them all, and incurred no expenses at all in procuring the original manuscripts.

The published papers were not immediately popular but gradually gained acceptance throughout England and Europe. Eventually, a copy of the papers came into the hands of one of the greatest scientists of the day, the Count de Buffon of France. He and his colleague, Mr. Dalibard, translated the papers into French and had them printed and distributed throughout Paris. My ideas about electricity gave great offense to Professor Nollet, France's greatest electrical scientist and science tutor for the royal family. He had previously published his own theory of electricity—at odds with my own—and it had won great approval throughout his country. He scoffed at the idea that this new theory came from such a place as America and claimed it was a fabrication by his enemies in Paris who wished to see his theories discredited.

Gradually, he was assured that there really existed in Philadelphia a person by the name of Benjamin Franklin who actually conducted these experiments. In response to me, he published some letters, addressed primarily to me, publicly defending his theory and attacking the scientific accuracy of my experiments and the theory I deduced from them. When I read his letters, I immediately began writing a response to his criticisms but decided to put the document aside after reflecting on the situation. After all, my published papers contained a full description of my experiments for anyone who wished to replicate any experiment and verify its claim. By the rules of science, if it could not be replicated, it could not be seriously defended. Further, I had offered my theory as more of a speculation than a dogmatic assertion of the facts. As a result I had little, if any, real territory to defend at present.

Our dispute was further complicated by the fact that it was being conducted across two languages. Professor Nollet had already criticized me on a matter that was in reality an error of translation. Why continue an already heated correspondence and give further chance for mistranslation? I thus decided to let my papers defend themselves. I thought it wiser to spend what little time I could spare from my official business conducting and publishing new experiments rather than fighting about those already past. So I never answered Nollet's criticism and I am yet to regret my silence on the matter. My friend Jean-Baptiste Le Roy of the Royal Academy of Sciences in France took it upon himself to refute Nollet's arguments. My papers were ultimately translated into Italian, German, and Latin and my theory was, in time, universally adopted by the scientists of Europe in preference to Professor Nollet's theory. Nollet lived to see himself the last believer in his theory, with the exception of his student and disciple Mr. Brisson.

Another name associated with electricity, Thomas Edison, was sometimes referred to as the "Benjamin Franklin of the 19th Century." Whereas Franklin eschewed patents, Edison still holds the record for the most patents granted—1,093 to be exact.

I had proposed several experiments in my book and the success of one of them gave the book a sudden burst of publicity. Mr. Dalibard and Mr. de Lor both drew lightning from the clouds, fascinating the French public. An experimental scientist and frequent lecturer, Mr. de Lor used pointed metal rods to replicate what he called "The Philadelphia Experiments." He performed them before the king and his court and, later, all the curious of Paris flocked to see them. At almost the same time, I conducted my own experiments with lightning using a kite outside of Philadelphia. The success of both these experiments gave me great pleasure. Rather than waste space on more details here, interested readers can find both in the histories of electricity.

The story would not be complete without my detailing the change of opinion about me in England. An English physician, Dr. Wright, traveled in Paris and noticed the high regard the French had for my ideas about electricity. He wrote to a friend in London—a member of the Royal Society—pointing this out and noting that the French were amazed that my work had received so little notice in England. On hearing this, the Royal Society reconsidered my letters at which they first had laughed. My case was sealed when an electrical expert, Dr. Watson, presented a summary of all my work before the members and noted its significance to the field. His summary was printed in their *Transactions* and several members, most notably Mr. Canton, soon replicated the experiments in England, drawing lightning from the clouds with a pointed rod.

To their credit, the Royal Society made an about-face and soon made amends to me for the poor treatment they had given me earlier. Without my even making application, they voted me a member of the Society and even excused me from paying the required initiation fee of 25 guineas. Since that time, they have forwarded their *Transactions* to me free of charge. On top of this, they presented me with the gold medal of Sir Godfrey Copley for the year 1753, their highest honor. The president of the Royal Society, Lord Macclesfield, gave me great tribute in his speech when the prize was announced.

CHAPTER 78

Holding Fast to Principle

Another new governor comes to Pennsylvania bound by the same restrictions as his predecessors. That is, he would be punished financially should he not follow the orders of the Penn family in London. In this chapter, Franklin shows us the strength required to hold firm to one's principles. To his credit, he avoids personal attacks and makes clear his basic principles and his commitment to a fair resolution to the matter. Beyond this, Franklin remains resolute in the face of what, if not a bribe, would have been at least a handsome public reward for turning aside from his duties. It is an impressive display of personal integrity and a reminder to be on your guard when you are honored by someone; you can be taken advantage of when flattered as easily as when you are angered.

OUR NEW GOVERNOR, CAPTAIN DENNY, BROUGHT the Copley medal with him when he sailed over from England. He presented it to me at his official reception hosted by the City of Philadelphia. In front of everyone gathered for the event, he gave me the medal accompanied by a public statement of the great respect he had for me as a man of established character. When the drinks were being poured after dinner, he took me aside into a quieter room and said that everyone in England had encouraged him to make friends with me quickly. He was told that I not only gave sound advice but that my counsel, if heeded, would most certainly make his administration more effective. He desired nothing more, he claimed, than to cultivate a good relationship with me and assured me that he stood ready to assist me to the extent his powers allowed.

He also told me that the Penn family wished only the best for Pennsylvania. Therefore, it would be to everyone's benefit—especially mine—if the longstanding opposition to the tax exemptions on the Penn family's properties was put aside and harmony restored between the Penns and the people of the province. If anyone could bring this about, he claimed, it would be Benjamin Franklin, and I could very well expect to receive proper acknowledgement and even compensation should it occur. Another decanter of Madeira wine was sent to us from the other room, and the governor poured it in bountiful quantities. The suggestions and promises flew faster from his mouth as the volume of wine grew in his glass.

> Principle helps us make the right decision when pressures might tempt us to do otherwise. When Wendy's Hamburgers was falsely accused by a customer of having a fingertip served in a bowl of chili, company leadership held fast to principle as the incident was investigated. The accusation was proven to be false.

I listened politely to the governor and then gave him the following answer. With thanks to God, my financial security was such that I was in no need of favors from the Penn family. Beyond this, as a member of the Assembly, it would be wrong of me to accept any from them. That said, I informed him that I had no personal conflict whatsoever with the Penn family. Should they propose a bill for the good of the people of Pennsylvania, they will find me a ready champion. My previous opposition to the Penn family had been based on principle rather than any personal hostility. Their previous bills were clearly intended to serve only the interests of the Penn family and treated the people of Pennsylvania unjustly. Further, I would continue to oppose any proposals that were fundamentally unjust. I thanked him for the kind words he had for me and let him know that he could certainly rely on me to provide him the desired advice for making his administration an effective one. At the same time, I expressed my hope that, in contrast to his predecessors, the Penn family had sent him to us without threatening to ruin him financially should he disobey any of their orders.

At that time, he gave no response as to whether the Penns had bridled him with such burdensome restrictions. When the time came for him to do business with the Assembly, however, it was clear that nothing had changed. The Penns still requested exemptions, the Assembly still opposed them, and the conflict continued. I remained active in the opposition and kept my station as the one in charge of responding to the governor's remarks. All my work is a matter of public record, including the Assembly's formal request for Governor Denny's instructions from the Penn family and our remarks about them.

> POOR RICHARD ONCE SAID, "LOVE YOUR ENEMIES, FOR THEY TELL YOU YOUR FAULTS."

As with his predecessor, no personal hostility arose between Governor Denny and me. We often spent time together, he being a man of letters who had seen much of the world. Our every conversation was pleasing and entertaining. He was the first to inform me that my old friend James Ralph was still alive and thought to be one of the best political writers in England. He had been employed during a dispute between the Prince of Wales and the King, and obtained a pension of 300 pounds per year from the Crown in return for his promise to stay out of politics—a compliment to his effectiveness, as it were. His prose was thought as good as anyone's but he had failed miserably in his quest to be a poet. In fact, he suffered the humiliation of having had his verse publicly criticized by a leading poet of the day, Alexander Pope.

But let's get back to the story. The Assembly had sent a bill to the governor for approval. This bill granted a sum of 60,000 pounds for the King's use (in matters of defense, of course). Ten thousand pounds of this sum were earmarked to be used at the discretion of General Braddock's successor, the General Lord Loudoun. As we expected, the governor refused to sign our bill, claiming that it went against his instructions not to tax the Penns' landholding in raising these funds. The Assembly concluded that the Penn family stubbornly insisted on shackling its appointed officials with instructions fundamentally opposed not only to the interest of the people but also to the service of the Crown. As a result, the Assembly resolved to take their petition directly to the King and appointed me to represent them in this undertaking.

I made arrangements with Captain Morris to sail on the next mail boat between New York and London. Just as my baggage was put on board the vessel, the General Lord Loudoun arrived in Philadelphia for the express purpose, he announced, of finding resolution between the governor and the Assembly so as not to impede His Majesty's service. He called a meeting between the governor and me to hear both sides of the conflict and I was obliged to attend. Accordingly, we met and laid our positions before him. I recited what was already in the public record in our defense and the governor pointed to his instructions, the bond he had given to observe them, and the financial ruin he could expect if he disobeyed.

During our talks, Governor Denny signaled a willingness to go against the Penns if he could do so with the general's support. Loudoun looked as though he would choose this course of action but abandoned the idea at the last minute, much to my disappointment. In the end, he chose to strong-arm the Assembly into compliance, declaring that he would provide none of the King's troops for the defense of the frontier. I thus brought back the message to the Assembly that if we did not continue to provide for our own defense, then our people would continue in danger of attack from the enemy.

I then drafted a set of resolutions and presented them to the Assembly. In these we declared our basic rights, among them the right to self-defense. Further, we did not relinquish our claim to these rights in this threatening set of circumstances. Rather, we were forced to suspend the exercise of them for the time being, and we did so under great protest. Along with this public statement, the Assembly agreed to drop their original bill and draft another, once again exempting the Penns' estate and saving the governor from financial ruin. Of course, the governor signed it immediately and I was now free to resume my trip to London to plead our case before the King. Unfortunately, the mail ship had sailed during the delay with Lord Loudoun, taking my baggage along with it. This loss was offset only by a few words of thanks from the general for my services. More irritating still, he took all the credit for breaking the impasse when all he really did was maintain the status quo and cause me great inconvenience about which I have more to say shortly.

CHAPTER 79

The Impact of Indecisive Leadership

Franklin has showcased a variety of poor leaders and poor leadership styles throughout the autobiography. As he draws them, Governor Morris loved conflict too much; Governor Denny was but a lackey; General Braddock was too proud; and here we learn about Lord Loudoun's indecisiveness and how it adversely affected many good people. Every character in the autobiography is there for a reason. Franklin understood the power of a good example, but he also understood the power of a bad one. I believe that Franklin included these characters to illustrate ineffective public leadership.

GENERAL LORD LOUDOUN SET OUT FOR NEW YORK ahead of me. Two additional mail ships remained in port awaiting his command to sail. He informed me that one would sail soon, and I asked him to tell me the precise time of its departure that I might not miss another vessel through any fault of my own. "I have announced that she'll set sail next Saturday," he responded. "However, privately I'll tell you that if you are there by Monday morning you'll find her still in port, but do not delay any longer than this." Due to some unforeseen delays at a ferry as I traveled to New York, I did not arrive there until Monday at noon. I suspected that I had missed the boat once again, as the wind was fair that day. I was pleased to discover that she was still in the harbor, however, and would not sail until the next day.

You would think that I was now on the very verge of making my much delayed voyage to England, but I was yet to learn about Lord Loudoun's character—indecision being one of its strongest features. I arrived in New York at the beginning of April, yet we did not sail until nearly the end of June. These two mail ships had been in port a long time and were kept there in hopes of receiving some letters from the general which were always "to be ready tomorrow." A third mail ship arrived and she was detained along with the first two in port. They brought news of a fourth ship due to arrive before we were expected to sail.

Of course, ours was expected to sail first as it had been in port the longest. All three were full of passengers, and some of these had become extremely impatient about the delay. Merchants throughout the colonies grew uneasy about their business letters. It being a time of war, some had ordered more insurance and their risk increased along with the delay. Beyond this, they had put orders in the mail for autumn goods, expecting the ships to sail in early April! The anxiety of the passengers and merchants mattered little, however, as his lordship's letters were just not ready. Amazingly, whoever visited the general always seemed to find him at his desk with pen in hand. We could only conclude that he must have to write an incredibly large number of letters.

I went to the general one morning to pay my respects. In his receiving room I found a messenger from Philadelphia, a Mr. Innis, who had came to deliver a packet of letters from Governor Denny to the general. Along with these, he delivered to me some letters from my friends in Philadelphia. This gave me reason to inquire about his return plans and where he lodged so that I might send some letters back with him. He informed me that he had been ordered to come back the next day at nine o'clock in the morning to retrieve the general's answer to the governor's letters and that he would set off immediately for Philadelphia from there.

> POOR RICHARD ONCE SAID, "CHANGING COUNTRIES OR BEDS, CURES NEITHER A BAD MANAGER NOR A FEVER."

Thus, I wrote my responses immediately and put them in his hands later that same day.

Two weeks later I met him once again in the general's receiving room. "Back again so soon, Mr. Innis?" I said. "Back?" he exclaimed. "I haven't even left yet!" He went on to tell me that he had been ordered back every morning at nine o'clock for the past two weeks to receive the general's letters for the governor and they were still not ready. I shared with Mr. Innis our observation that the general seemed to be at his desk constantly writing letters. "Yes," he replied, "but he is like St. George on the signs: always on horseback but never really riding anywhere!" Innis's observation seemed to be accurate. I learned later in England that General Loudoun lost his post for this very reason. William Pitt, the prime minister, replaced him with Generals Amherst and Wolfe, complaining that he never heard from him and never knew what he was doing.

CHAPTER 80

More on Poor Leadership

Franklin continues to explore Loudoun's poor leadership and its negative impact on so many. He also gives us a glimpse into Loudoun's character when matters of money take center stage. Loudoun's accusing Franklin of lining his own pockets during the war is most likely just a projection of Loudoun's own personal habits. The bill was only for the 17 pounds still owed Franklin at the end of Chapter 65. Nonetheless, Loudoun managed to both insult Franklin's character and refuse to reimburse an incredibly small amount of money.

OUR WAITING CONTINUED BUT WE STILL EXPECTED to sail any day since the general had given us no reason to believe otherwise. The three mail ships sailed down to the calm waters inside Sandy Hook to join the rest of the fleet there that stood ready to sail together across the Atlantic. All the passengers thought it best to stay aboard the ships, fearing they might be left behind if the ships sailed without notice. We stayed in Sandy Hook about six weeks, if I remember aright. We consumed all the food we had on board the ship and had to purchase a new round of stores for the trip.

Finally, the fleet left New York but was not yet wholly free to sail to England. With the general and his troops along, the fleet steered toward the French stronghold at Louisberg, which guarded the entrance to the St. Lawrence River, with the intent to begin a siege and take that fortress. The mail ships were ordered to stay alongside the general's ship in order to receive even more of his letters when they were ready. We sailed north for five days before receiving permission to part. Our ship turned toward England, but the other two mail ships were detained with the general all the way to Halifax, where the general decided to engage his troops in military exercises attacking replica forts. Believe it or not, the general then decided not to lay siege to Louisberg and returned to New York, diverting with him all his troops, the two remaining mail ships, and all their passengers! The French and Indians had taken advantage of his absence to capture Fort William Henry at Lake George, on the frontier of colonial New York, and they massacred many of the troops there after they surrendered.

Some time later in London, I happened to meet Captain Bonnell, the commander of one of those two mail ships. He told me that after he had been delayed the first month, he notified the general that the ship had grown foul below her waterline. As these growths can significantly hinder the speed at which his ship could sail, he asked leave to take the ship ashore and clean her bottom. When the general asked how long this would take, Captain Bonnell's reply was three days. To this the general replied, "If you can do it in one day, I give my permission. Otherwise, you may not, for you will certainly sail the day after tomorrow." He never obtained the general's permission, despite being detained in port a full three months more. In London I also met a passenger from Captain Bonnell's ship. The general had so enraged this fellow, through his detaining the ships so long in New York and then taking them to Halifax and back again, that he swore he would sue for damages. I don't know whether he did or not, but I was amazed by the list of damages he laid before me that day.

At the time, I wondered how such a man as Lord Loudoun came to be appointed as commander-in-chief of His Majesty's army. Having seen more of the world since that time, my wonder is now much diminished; I realize the variety of ways one can obtain such a position. General Shirley, upon whom fell the command of the army after Braddock's death, would have made a better go of it than Loudoun, in my opinion. Loudoun's campaign in 1757 was pointless, expensive, and a complete disgrace to all. Though Shirley was not brought up to be a soldier, he was both sensible and aware of his limitations. He was not above taking good advice from others, crafting a plan from it, and executing it quickly.

Loudoun, in contrast, left the colonies defenseless and lost Fort William Henry while he drilled his troops in the safety of Halifax. Beyond this, he angered merchants across the colonies—and weakened our trade—by ordering a lengthy embargo on the export of any goods. He claimed such an embargo would keep the goods out of enemy hands. In reality, the embargo served only to beat down our merchants' prices to the ultimate benefit of the competition. Rumor held that Lord Loudoun enjoyed a cut of these profits, but that has never been proven. At length, Loudoun lifted the embargo but failed to send proper notice to the ships waiting in Charleston. As a result, the Carolina fleet was delayed nearly three months longer than the others, their bottoms so damaged by the worm that many of them were wrecked before they made it back to London.

> POOR RICHARD ONCE SAID, "HE THAT WOULD CATCH FISH, MUST VENTURE HIS BAIT."

Given his lack of professional training, I suspect Shirley was sincerely pleased to be relieved of the command of so large an army. I attended the party given to Lord Loudoun by the City of New York when he arrived to take command of the troops. Although passed over for the job, Shirley was there also. A large number of officers, citizens, and others attended the event. The crowd was so large that chairs were borrowed from all over the neighborhood. One of these chairs was particularly low and fell by chance to Shirley. I noticed it when I sat by him and remarked, "Sir, they have given you too low a seat." He replied, "It's not a bother, Mr. Franklin. I find the lowest seat the easiest to fill."

While detained in New York those months, I received the last of the accounting records for the provisions I had furnished General Braddock. I presented them to Lord Loudoun and asked to be paid the balance due. He had the records carefully checked by the appropriate officer, who certified them to be right. Upon hearing this, the general promised to give me an order to receive the money from the paymaster. Not surprisingly, this was continually delayed, though I made many an appointment to pick it up. Having still not received it at the point of my departure, Loudoun informed me that he had reconsidered and decided not to mix his accounts with those of his predecessors. He told me to show my records to the treasury when I arrived in London and I would be paid immediately.

Offering a reason for prompter payment, I mentioned the large and unplanned expense I had incurred during this rather lengthy delay in New York. I suggested that it was not right that I should be put to even more trouble and delay in obtaining the money I had advanced the general, charging no commission for my service. "My good sir," he said, "there's no need trying to persuade us that you're not profiteering somewhere in this deal. We understand such military affairs better than you think and know that everyone involved in supplying an army finds a way of filling his own pockets in the process." I assured him that this was not the case but he did not appear to believe me. I have since learned that enormous fortunes have indeed been made in this manner. My balance, however, remains unpaid to this day.

CHAPTER 81

The Slowest Ship

This is one of my favorite stories in the entire autobiography. Franklin uses the tale of the reorganization aboard a sailing ship to remind us of the importance of clear thinking and good leadership. Along the way, he tells us once again that effort, initiative, and creativity can make up for some of the worst beginnings.

BEFORE WE SAILED, THE CAPTAIN OF OUR VESSEL, Captain Lutwidge, had bragged a good deal about his ship's swiftness. When we got out on the ocean, however, she proved the slowest of the 96 vessels in our fleet. He suffered a great deal of humiliation because of this and offered many explanations as to the cause of the problem. One day we happened to pass by another ship almost as slow as ours—and let me emphasize "almost"—as even this ship gained on us. With this point of reference, the captain ordered all 40 people aboard to the rear of the boat and to stand as near to the back of the ship as possible. As we stood there, the ship shifted in the water a bit and soon left this neighboring ship far behind. This proved what the captain had guessed to be true: Too much weight had been loaded in the front of the ship, causing her to drag. Going below, we learned that all the barrels of fresh water had been loaded near the front of the ship. The captain ordered these barrels moved more to the rear of the ship. When they were, the ship recovered her balance and proved to be one of the speediest vessels in the fleet.

His pride now restored, the captain informed some of the passengers that his ship had once reached a speed of 13 knots. Another of our passengers, a naval captain named Kennedy, heard this remark and contended that such a speed was impossible. He had never known a ship to sail at that speed and suggested that there must have been a mathematical error when the speed was measured with the log line. To settle the matter, the two captains made a bet with one another to be settled when sufficient wind existed to conduct the experiment. In the meantime, Captain Kennedy meticulously examined the ship's sailing and speed records. Satisfied with their accuracy, he determined that he should throw the log line himself to test the speed when the time came. Many days later, a strong wind blew fair and fresh in our direction. Captain Lutwidge informed Captain Kennedy that the ship was now at top speed and should be found to be sailing at thirteen knots. Kennedy, in turn, threw the log line, checked his figures, and paid Lutwidge the money he owed for losing the wager.

I share these two stories to make the following point: Common wisdom dictates that ship-building is an imperfect craft, and that it can never be known whether a ship will sail well until she is in the water. Builders can construct a ship according to a good plan, but she can prove quite dull once upon the sea. But origin is not destiny. Variations in performance across vessels might be explained other ways.

> POOR RICHARD ONCE SAID, "HE THAT RESOLVES TO MEND HEREAFTER, RESOLVES NOT TO MEND NOW."

Almost every captain has a different method of loading his ship, and personal preferences extend to the rigging and sailing of the vessel as well. The very same ship under the command of one captain may sail much better or much worse under the command of a different captain. One man builds her hull, another rigs her sails, still a third loads and commands her upon the water. None of these three can benefit from the wisdom of the others but each must do his best with the materials he is given. As a result, we must be very careful in judging a person who often works wonders though saddled by the problems of others who are no longer present.

These complexities extend even to the operation of sailing when at sea. In my travels, I have witnessed vastly different judgments from the officers who commanded the different shifts throughout the day. Although the wind stayed the same all day, one would trim the sails sharper and the other flatter, and there was often no rule to guide them other than personal preference. We are entering into an Age of Experiments, and I think we would all benefit from a set of experiments to improve the science of sailing. For example, one experiment might determine what shape of the hull maximizes the speed of the vessel. Another might help determine the best placement and dimensions for the masts. Continuing this idea, the shape and quantity of the sails should be tested. Finally, as has already been shown here, we should also determine guidelines for the proper loading of sailing ships. Though I might not live to see it, I am convinced that some brilliant scientist will take the challenge, and I wish this person great success.

Like Franklin, modern entrepreneurs and businesspeople remain fascinated with the future of travel, especially space travel. Recently, both Microsoft co-founder Paul Allen and Amazon.com founder Jeff Bezos both invested money into private space travel ventures.

CHAPTER 82

No Substitute for Integrity

Franklin approached England with some terrible knowledge. Fifty years prior to his crossing, four British ships, homeward bound after a battle with the French in the Mediterranean, struck the Scilly Islands off the southwest tip of England, killing 2,000 officers and sailors. It happened on the night of October 22, 1707, and was the Titanic *of the 18th century: a disaster with major cultural impact especially tragic because it occurred in British waters. In this final chapter, Franklin and his fellow passengers arrive in England barely avoiding the same fate. Once again, his narrative about how a careless watchman almost wrecks the ship suggests that management systems—no matter how carefully designed—are no substitute for personal integrity. At the close of this section, Franklin fittingly provides the image of a curtain rising on a new period of his life. Indeed, his trip to London in 1757 would prove to be a distinct break from his past.*

WE WERE CHASED BY FRENCH WARSHIPS SEVERAL times during our passage across the Atlantic but outran every ship that tried to overtake us. After 30 days we were close enough to land to hit bottom with our sounding equipment. After some good observations, Captain Lutwidge thought us to be so near to our port in Falmouth that, if we continued to sail through the night, we might find ourselves at the mouth of the harbor the next morning. A night approach offered the additional benefit of security from privateers, who often cruised near the entrance to the harbor to pick off incoming ships.

The wind was fresh and fair, so we raised all the sails we could and headed toward the harbor as night fell. Captain Lutwidge set our course—or so he thought—to pass wide of that rugged group of rocks known as the Scilly Islands. However, at times there is a very strong current in the channel between Ireland and Wales that deceives even the best sailors and causes them to crash upon the Scilly Islands. This phenomenon caused the loss of four out of six ships in Sir Clowdisley Shovell's Squadron in 1707, and it also probably caused the great scare I'll describe next.

The captain placed a watchman at the front of the ship that night. The crew called regularly to the watchman, "Look well out before there!" and he regularly answered back, "Ay! Ay!" But he may have answered mechanically with his eyes shut and half asleep because he did not see the lighthouse that was right in front of our vessel. The men at the helm and the rest of the watchmen could not see this light because it was blocked by the sails. The ship just happened to catch a large wave and the lighthouse suddenly became visible to the rest of the crew, who raised an enormous alarm on deck. We were right on top of it; from my vantage point on deck the light was as large as a wagon wheel.

Being midnight, our captain was fast asleep below deck, but Captain Kennedy, being awake, noticed the danger. He jumped upon deck and ordered the vessel to turn into the wind without trimming any of the sails—a dangerous maneuver that runs the risk of breaking the masts. His gamble carried us clear, however, and we escaped what was a certain shipwreck. We were seconds from sailing full force into the rocks on which the lighthouse sat. This incident left me with a strong impression of the usefulness of lighthouses. I resolved there and then to encourage the building of more lighthouses in America—should I live long enough to return there.

The next morning our soundings suggested to us that we were very near our port, but a thick fog hid the land from our sight. The fog began to rise about nine o'clock and lifted from the water like a curtain at a playhouse. As this curtain lifted, we beheld the town of Falmouth, the vessels in its harbor, and the green

> POOR RICHARD ONCE SAID, "READER, I WISH THEE HEALTH, WEALTH, HAPPINESS, AND MAY KIND HEAVEN THY YEAR'S INDUSTRY BLESS."

fields all around. This is such a pleasing spectacle when you've had nothing but the view of the endless ocean day after day for the past month. The view is even more pleasant when one has crossed the sea during a time of war and can now leave those anxieties behind.

———><●<———

AFTERWORD

The Rest of the Story

*T*he autobiography does not end here, but our story does. Franklin continued writing for a few more pages, describing his five-and-a-half-year stay in London. During these years he fought and won a painstakingly slow legal battle with the Penn family over the taxation of their estate holdings. If we include the latest possible event he mentions in his autobiography, he ended the text when he was 57 years old. This version of the autobiography ends with Franklin just 51 years old.

We also end where we began: Franklin mentioned this "trip to England" in the second sentence of his autobiography (see page 3, second sentence of Chapter 1). Much of his life remained, and it had already begun to shift away from matters of business to matters of politics. This second trip to London proved a turning point and public duties began to dominate his life. He lived another 33 years, during which he realized some of his most significant accomplishments.

Since this text ends with his arrival in England on July 27, 1757, it might be useful to offer a brief timeline of events describing the remainder of Franklin's life.

1758: Advocates case for Pennsylvania Assembly in dispute with Penn family; visits ancestral homes in Ecton and Banbury, collecting genealogical information; meets variety of luminaries including David Hume, author of *A Treatise of Human Nature.*

1759: Receives honorary Doctor of Laws degree from University of St. Andrews in Scotland and is thereafter referred to as "Dr. Franklin"; meets Adam Smith, who would later write *The Wealth of Nations.*

1760: Continues to advocate in Assembly dispute; meets Dr. Samuel Johnson.

1761: Continues to advocate dispute; attends the coronation of King George III.

1762: Receives honorary Doctor of Civil Laws from Oxford; invents musical instrument known as glass armonica; son William made royal governor of New Jersey; leaves London and returns to Philadelphia in November.

1763: Inspects post offices throughout the colonies; works with charity schools for blacks in Philadelphia.

1764: Elected Speaker of Pennsylvania Assembly but loses post later that year; returns to London to act as agent for Assembly to oppose Stamp Act in Parliament.

1765: Stamp Act becomes law in England and new taxes cause riots and much dissent in the colonies; agitates for repeal of Stamp Act.

1766: Sells print shop to longtime partner David Hall; succeeds in getting Stamp Act repealed and becomes preeminent voice in England for the American colonies.

1767: Continues campaign against colonial taxation; meets King Louis XV of France.

1768: Writes brief history of relations between American colonies and Britain; publishes charts showing the course of the Gulf Stream in the Atlantic Ocean; appointed agent for Georgia Assembly.

1769: Appointed agent for New Jersey House of Representatives; wife suffers a stroke and her health begins to deteriorate.

1770: Elected agent for Massachusetts House of Representatives.

1771: Tours Ireland and Scotland extensively; begins writing his autobiography.

1772: Concludes that slavery is inherently evil and morally unjust; frees and releases all slaves in his control; secretly obtains controversial Hutchinson letters.

1773: Hutchinson letter controversy spreads through Massachusetts House and London; Franklin accused of theft and treason in controversy.

1774: Viciously attacked and publicly humiliated in Hutchinson letter hearings; works to negotiate peace between England and the colonies as tensions escalate; wife dies of stroke in December.

1775: Leaves London and returns to Philadelphia; chosen delegate to Second Continental Congress; King George proclaims colonies to be in rebellion.

1776: Helps draft Declaration of Independence and signs; appointed commissioner to France by Congress and sails for Paris in October.

1777: Receives aid from France for colonial revolution and forges formal alliance after news of British defeat at Saratoga.

1778: France goes to war against Britain and gives more financial aid to Congress; meets Voltaire.

1779: Spain declares war on Britain; more financial aid given by France.

1780: Feuds with John Adams in peace negotiations between France and Britain.

1781: Cornwallis surrenders to Washington at Yorktown; serious peace negotiations begin.

1782: Britain formally recognizes the United States Congress; receives more financial aid from France.

1783: Peace treaties signed between United States and Great Britain; witnesses first manned balloon flights.

1784: Peace treaty with Great Britain formally ratified; continues writing autobiography.

1785: Invents bifocal glasses; after nine years abroad finally returns to Philadelphia and given a hero's welcome; elected president of Supreme Executive Council of Pennsylvania, his last public office.

1786: Expands his house on Market Street in Philadelphia to include a large dining room and a 4,000-volume library.

1787: Becomes president of Pennsylvania Society for Promoting the Abolition of Slavery; attends federal Constitutional Convention as Pennsylvania delegate.

1788: Continues writing his autobiography; writes last will and testament; resigns as president of Supreme Executive Council of Pennsylvania, ending remarkable career in public service.

1789: Writes and signs first protest against slavery given to American Congress; makes philanthropic bequests to Boston and Philadelphia.

1790: Dies at home of pleurisy on April 17 after a lengthy illness.

I close this volume by once again pointing to Franklin's original autobiography. Now that you have a basic understanding of Franklin's story, go back and read it in his words. My modern adaptation can make the *Autobiography* more accessible but cannot capture the sparkle and wit of the original composition. For many years, the most authoritative edition was the Norton Critical Edition of *Benjamin Franklin's Autobiography,* edited by J.A. Leo Lemay and Paul M. Zall (W.W. Norton & Company, 1986). More recently, the Editors of *The Papers of Benjamin Franklin* assembled a very helpful volume with *The Autobiography of Benjamin Franklin (Second Edition)* (Yale University Press, 2003).

Beyond the autobiography, interested readers might also enjoy Paul M. Zall's *Franklin on Franklin* (University of Kentucky Press, 2001) in which Zall collects all of Franklin's autobiographical writings throughout his life. Zall's text is a must for those who want to read about all of Franklin's life in his own words. Zealous readers will also enjoy the Library of America's volume on Franklin simply entitled *Benjamin Franklin: Writings* (Library of America, 1987) edited by J.A. Leo Lemay. This is the best one-volume collection of Franklin's writings in existence.

Acknowledgments

First and foremost, thanks to everyone at Entrepreneur Press—especially my longtime editor Jere Calmes and Leanne Harvey, Director of Marketing. Next, thanks to everyone at my literary agency, Yates & Yates, and especially to Curtis Yates for his wise counsel. Deepest gratitude goes to Karen Billipp of Eliot House Productions for creating such a wonderful interior design. Thanks to my Baylor colleague, Dr. Sharyn Dowd, for her help in sharpening the sections on Franklin's religious heritage and religious thinking. Thanks to Robin Harris and Grant Case for reading through the early drafts and giving helpful recommendations (especially for Chapter 65, Grant). Special thanks to my graduate assistants, Akshay Joshi and Shilpa Vasandani, for locating numerous useful Franklin resources and for giving me an international perspective on Franklin's story. Finally, deepest gratitude to Baylor University for granting me a research leave in the Fall 2003, when I lived in the Northeast. This gave me the chance to do the bulk of the work on this book in the very places where Franklin lived.

Index